Praise for
MIRACLES EVERY DAY

"*Miracles Every Day* is an astonishing book not just because the story of a man's ability to heal is real, but because you can sense the truth of this man's power and grace on every page. This book renews your faith in prayer, healing, and the Divine."

—Caroline Myss, author of *Defy Gravity* and *Anatomy of the Spirit*

"We read a lot about spiritual and miraculous healing in the Gospels and very little about it in the modern world. We all have a need for healing. This book will help you work out what healing you need."

—Matthew Kelly, *New York Times* bestselling author of
Rediscovering Catholicism and *The Rhythm of Life*

"I could not help but be deeply impressed by the awesome healings in *Miracles Every Day* and the love of God and neighbor that runs through all of Dr. Nemeh's work. I hope people of all backgrounds, and especially people in the medical field, will read this book. It can enrich our lives and open our minds to the awesome goodness and healing love that has touched so many lives."

—Father Joseph F. Girzone, author of *Joshua: A Parable for Today* and
Jesus: A New Understanding of God's Son

MIRACLES
EVERY
DAY

The Story of
One Physician's Inspiring Faith
and the
Healing Power of Prayer

Maura Poston Zagrans

DOUBLEDAY RELIGION
New York London Toronto Sydney Auckland

ⅭD

DOUBLEDAY

Copyright © 2010 by Maura Zagrans

Published in the United States by Doubleday Religion,
an imprint of the Crown Publishing Group,
a division of Random House, Inc., New York.
www.crownpublishing.com
www.doubledayreligion.com

DOUBLEDAY and the DD colophon are registered
trademarks of Random House, Inc.

Library of Congress Cataloging-in-Publication Data
Zagrans, Maura Poston.
Miracles every day : the story of one physician's inspiring faith and the healing
power of prayer / Maura Poston Zagrans. — 1st ed.
p.   cm.
Includes bibliographical references and index.
1. Nemeh, Issam. 2. Christian physicians—Ohio—Biography. 3. Spiritual healing.
4. Miracles. I. Title.
BR1725.N425 Z34 2010
234'.131092—dc22
[B]   2009043923

ISBN 978-0-385-53181-8
PRINTED IN THE UNITED STATES OF AMERICA

Design by Jennifer Ann Daddio / Bookmark Design & Media Inc.

1   3   5   7   9   10   8   6   4   2
First Edition

This book is dedicated with love to

my parents,

KITTY AND PAUL POSTON,

for the miracle of a happy childhood;

my daughters,

BRITTANY, JACKIE, AND JULI,

for the miracle of their friendship;

and my editor,

GARY JANSEN,

for the many miracles he brought to this book.

Where there is great love there are always miracles.

—WILLA CATHER

Contents

PART TWO

ANSWER "THE CALL"

PART THREE

VISIONS OF FAMILY

PART FOUR

FAITH AND WORKS

Author's Note

This is a book about faith, prayer, and the power of love. It is also the true story of a man who has fused these elements into his daily life, a physician whose maxim really is "miracles every day."

Issam Nemeh, M.D., has pursued a lifelong calling to demonstrate the healing power of love, and the story of his submission to a cause greater than himself is inspiring.

People tend to look at Dr. Nemeh from slightly different viewpoints. Some see in his career proof that one man can make a difference in the world. Others say he gave them hope against all odds. Some say he saved their lives, while others say he saved their souls. What is it about this humble, limelight-averse person that arouses such passion?

I first met Dr. Nemeh and his wife, Kathy, who plays an integral role in Dr. Nemeh's ministry, in a French pastry and catering shop owned by our mutual friend Charlene Kalo on Christmas Eve 2006. We shook hands and spoke for a few minutes, an exchange that remains vivid in my mind because the impressions conveyed to me were extraordinary. Kathy was warmth and liveliness; the doctor was compassion and gentleness. I never dreamed I would soon be writing a book about them.

I knew almost nothing about the Nemehs. Charlene had once mentioned something to me about their being involved in a gathering of ten thousand people, but as she reminisced about the day I stared at her uncomprehendingly. I really didn't know what she was talking about.

The husband of one of my dearest friends was a patient of Dr. Nemeh's, and he had talked about the doctor with reverence and love.

Other than those two tiny connections, I was a blank slate. I never saw televised broadcasts about Dr. Nemeh because twenty-five years earlier I had traded television-watching time for quality time to read and be with my children. Healing services, falling in the spirit, and being prayed over were completely foreign to me.

When I began working on the book, I may have been disadvantaged by a steep learning curve, but what I had going for me was an objective, unbiased perspective. I logged thousands of hours of interview and observation time and eventually came to the conclusion that Dr. Nemeh's story should be told because it is authentic. I also came to understand why people feel so strongly about him and how it is he fulfills so many different functions for the people whose lives he has touched. This book, then, is about life journeys—his and theirs.

Dr. Nemeh insists God is the only healer, but he never imposes his beliefs on anyone. Just as a rose is a rose by any other name, so too is a miracle a miracle whether attributed to God or to love. The important point is that when Dr. Nemeh prays over a person the connection that occurs oftentimes initiates a change that leads to happiness and healing on many levels.

Every story related in this book is true and unembellished. Because it is not possible within the scope of one book to compile all the miracles associated with Dr. Nemeh's career, each account was selected as a representative of a *type* of patient or a *kind* of healing. A few names have been changed to protect people's privacy.

In May 2007 I attended a retreat at which Kathy Nemeh, during her remarks at the podium, told a charming story of calling her husband over to where she was jotting ideas for her speech on index cards. "Issam," she asked, "who *are* you? We've been married twenty-five years and you're still an enigma to me."

Issam turned on his heel, walked into another room, and returned carrying a painting of Jesus' Palm Sunday procession. He answered with a question of his own. "If you could be anyone in this picture, who would you be?" When she didn't comprehend his point, he explained, "I would want to be the one who is closest to Jesus. The one who is patiently carrying Jesus to the people: the donkey."

Dr. Nemeh sees himself as one who serves. The humility with which he has answered his calling stands as a reminder that we too can honor God by serving one another.

Part One

THE DAY
OF THE
TEN
THOUSAND

I.

A Vision Fulfilled

Ten thousand people came seeking not just a miracle. They came in search of *their* miracle.

On March 13, 2005, they came to Garfield Heights, Ohio, to Sts. Peter and Paul Catholic Church by private ambulance, in motorized lift vans, and in sedans displaying handicapped hangtags. They came alone and they came with families. They walked with heads held high and they hobbled through the parking lot on crutches. They stood in Disney World–long lines that snaked across a network of sidewalks crisscrossing the parish campus. They came looking for hope. They came looking for healing. At twenty-one degrees and with a piercing wind blowing, many would later recall the desperation of the day wrapped in a memory of brittle cold.

Constructed in the 1950s, the Romanesque church seats eight hundred beneath her graceful arches and towering columns. Painted murals and stained-glass windows depict St. Paul's conversion on the road to Damascus and the primacy of St. Peter, among other images. As caretakers pushed loved ones up the aisles, some in wheelchairs, some on hospital gurneys, hymns were being played by the pipe organist in the loft above. Canes, crutches, and walkers could be seen throughout the dense gathering, hard evidence of injuries, disease, or just the physical deterioration of old age. In the pews, bald children pressed close to their parents.

People entered the church filled with a mixture of faith and skepticism, trust and fear, acceptance and anger. They braved the frigid weather and then waited many hours inside, lured by a glimmer of hope that they might be released from the pain in their bodies and the suffering in their questioning souls. They came because they had heard that Dr. Issam Nemeh would lay his hands on each one of them, one person at a time, and say a prayer that each would be healed.

For Dr. Nemeh, this day was the culmination of years of hard work and sacrifice. Over the course of two decades he had laid the foundation for this moment by working as an anesthesiologist who sat beside his recovering patients in hushed hospital rooms, and then as an acupuncture practitioner in private practice. When Issam was fifteen years old he had a vision that he would share his gift of faith with thousands, but first he would have to form a solid base for this ministry with a medical practice.

Dr. Nemeh was a physician licensed by the State Medical Board of Ohio with specialties in anesthesiology and general surgery but switched midcareer to the practice of Meridian Regulatory Acupuncture. He says he made the career change in response to a message from God that said this new practice would give him time to work with people one on one. Indeed, patients have reported treatment sessions lasting one, two, and sometimes even three hours.

Many patients came to the doctor in a last-ditch effort, after having been told by mainstream medicine there was nothing more that could be done to alleviate their pain, treat their cancer, heal their handicaps, or save their lives. All the while the doctor was bent over his patients administering acupuncture, he prayed. Many patients received dramatic healings: tumors disappeared; multiple sclerosis melted away; vision returned to the blind and hearing to the deaf; migraines vanished; clinical depression was lifted; nerves were regenerated; learning disabilities vaporized; people relegated to wheelchairs stood and walked for the first time in years.

Through the years, when patients were restored to health after medical science had said cures were impossible, they wanted to share their stories with the media. Dr. Nemeh redirected them. He requested that they spread the word only to the sick and suffering. In the meantime, he waited for a sign from God that it was time to bring the praying from behind the closed doors of his practice out into the public forum.

Dr. Nemeh's acupuncture practice grew by means of word-of-mouth referrals from his patients. A nun living in Parma, Ohio, began hearing about Dr. Nemeh from people who came to her chapel to worship at her Wednesday night healing Masses. This feisty sixty-six-year-old born in County Mayo, Ireland, would herself become a patient. After the doctor helped Sister Monica Marie Navin, she proposed that Dr. Nemeh participate in celebrating her miracle with a Mass of Thanksgiving, after which he would pray over seventy-five invited guests, one at a time. And so it began.

Like a far-off stampede that is felt and heard before it is seen, word of the doctor's gift spread from the whispers of his patients, who told stories of their healings to loved ones and friends. One of those who caught word of what was going on was Emmy Award–winning Cleveland News Channel 5's lead anchor Ted Henry. He heard the rumblings, investigated, and in November 2004 broke the story of this quiet man whose touch was sought by many.

Intrigued by his initial investigation and the testimonials of astonishing cures coming from people from so many walks of life, Henry continued his research. He developed an eleven-part report that began airing on Cleveland's News Channel 5 on February 20, 2005. WEWS TV 5 cameras had filmed Cleveland Bishop Anthony M. Pilla celebrating a healing service liturgy at St. Mary's Chapel on the campus of St. Ignatius High School, and some weeks later Bishop Pilla granted Henry an interview in which he probed the bishop on the Catholic Church's official stance on miracles. In that interview Bishop Pilla explained, "It's clear in Catholic teaching that miracles are possible—that healing can take place. This is not just magic. We pray to God and then patiently and humbly we wait for God's response, which is always what's best for us."

Henry's report included video footage of Dr. Nemeh giving a lecture at Case Western Reserve University School of Medicine and praying at public healing services. Viewers did not see a bombastic, aggressive showman preaching and preening onstage before a congregation. What they saw was a quiet, dignified man praying in an atmosphere of solemn decorum, a gentleman in every sense of the word. In his interview, when Henry asked Bishop Pilla why he had chosen to sanction the doctor's work by officiating at the St. Mary's healing service, Bishop Pilla offered commentary on the style and motives of both Dr. Nemeh and his wife, Kathy. He said, "They're not looking for any sensationalism. They're not looking for any personal reward or praise or adulation. They're just doing this as part of their faith commitment, their belief that God can heal and that every person can be an instrument of that healing."

At the end of Ted Henry's nightly reports, TV 5 flashed a banner across the television screen detailing information about the next scheduled public healing service to be held immediately following the noon Mass on March 13 at Sts. Peter and Paul Catholic Church in Garfield Heights. City police, fire officials, and church personnel braced for a crowd they estimated would be somewhere between three thousand and four thousand people. Their estimate was off by as many as seven thousand.

2.

Plans

Two weeks before the healing service, Father Ted Marszal, pastor at Sts. Peter and Paul, and the parish's lead event coordinator, retired police officer Al Strnad, met with Kathy Nemeh and three of her volunteers to try to anticipate the needs of a crowd four to five times the capacity of the church, and to develop strategies to handle those needs. Diane Slovenski, the parish secretary, missed most of the dialogue because they had installed a new line to handle the deluge of calls requesting admission to the healing service, and that new phone never stopped ringing. Elaborate preparations were made for conducting the flow of traffic, including the establishment of a parking lot traffic control team. Maps giving directions to ten off-site parking facilities and area restaurants were printed so that they could be distributed to drivers who would have to be redirected from the church parking lot after it filled up. Homeowners and businesses in the neighborhood were alerted, and most everyone offered whatever parking facilities were at their disposal. Al conducted two instructional sessions to train 250 parishioners who volunteered for one-hour shifts. Yet when the day came, once the volunteers arrived at their posts many of them did not want to leave and go home. They were motivated by an overwhelming desire to serve. They also wanted to remain as long as possible in what they were experiencing as an intensely spiritual atmosphere. So Al then had to struggle with how to place these dozens of extra people into already overcrowded conditions.

Sts. Peter and Paul staff salted the sidewalks; overstocked the restrooms with paper towels, toilet paper, and cleaning supplies; and were poised to put in some overtime. They also prepared the school activity center, a combination athletics facility and social hall located across the courtyard from the church, by setting up five hundred folding chairs and a small but pretty altar on the stage in this cavernous room. Bishop Roger W. Gries was recruited to celebrate Mass in this makeshift chapel at noon. Throughout the day the building would provide shelter from the cold as people waited for space in the church pews to become available. Once inside the church, everyone would settle in for another long wait. Priests and chaplains from other parishes offered the sacrament of the anointing of the sick; they would go through several quarts of holy oil before the day ended.

The Nemehs had accepted an offer of assistance from Brecksville firefighter Lieutenant Patrick Coleman, who had received an instantaneous healing of an untreatable digestive disorder after a prayer from Dr. Nemeh at a service back in 2003. Kathy placed Patrick in charge of crowd control. He was the emissary and troubleshooter on behalf of the Nemeh ministry, the parallel of Al Strnad at Sts. Peter and Paul.

The Garfield Heights chief of police and fire chief both

planned to be on-site the entire day. To everyone's credit, preparations were so thorough the day would end without a single incident.

On the morning of the event, choppers hovered in the air and fed Cleveland's local news stations video of a constant crawl of traffic on the highway and lines of people streaming toward the church. Every Cleveland television station planted a live truck in the church parking lot, and reporters went live at each broadcast. When the six o'clock news announced that the doctor was still praying, Patrick faced a fresh onslaught of vehicles trying to find places to park.

After the numbered tickets had been collected and the traffic patterns analyzed from helicopter videotape, the Garfield Heights Police Department provided an estimate of how many people had made a pilgrimage to Sts. Peter and Paul Church that day. Everyone was astonished to learn that not three or four thousand but more than *ten* thousand people had descended upon the Garfield Heights parish.

Everyone, that is, but Dr. Nemeh. For him it was all simply part of God's plan.

3

The Plans Unfold

I ssam had told his wife, Kathy, when they were newlyweds that such a thing as this day at Sts. Peter and Paul would come to pass. He had confided that he had a mission to help bring people closer to God. Even so, as they pulled into the parking lot that morning, Kathy did not comprehend the chaos. Issam just shrugged. "I told you thousands would come," he said. Kathy felt a chill of recognition go through her. He *had* told her thousands would come. So *this* is what he had meant.

The day of the healing service Issam and Kathy arrived a little before the nine o'clock Mass. Father Ted Marszal was at the rectory to greet them. Kathy shivered in the cold as she and Issam unloaded the dinner she had prepared, enough food to feed a couple dozen volunteers.

Issam followed Father Ted from the rectory kitchen through an enclosed breezeway and into the sacristy. From behind the altar Issam gazed out on the packed church and thought, *These are God's chosen ones.* Thick wrestling mats lay on the floor behind the communion railing, where volunteers would usher people to stand for prayer. Ten chairs were placed in front of the first pew on either side of the aisle for those who did not have the strength to stand. Wheelchairs and hospital gurneys lined the wide center aisle, and the plan was for Dr. Nemeh to walk up and down the aisle and pray over those people.

Dr. Nemeh believed his job was to play a role in propelling each individual into a closer relationship with God. If it took a physical healing or miracle to accomplish this, so be it. This did not seem a daunting task to him; rather he thought of it as a privilege. He would pray to the Holy Spirit to forge a connection between each person and God. He would participate in each person's life journey, and, more important, everyone's spiritual journey, by surrendering his hands and his faith to God's purpose.

Father Ted had decided to adhere to the usual Sunday morning schedule of Masses offered at seven-thirty, nine, ten-thirty, and noon. When Al arrived at six that morning to place orange cones in the parking lot, he was surprised to find that there were people already inside the church. These early arrivals appeared to be willing to sit through four consecutive Masses so as not to lose their seats for the healing service. The church filled up so quickly that by ten o'clock Al and Patrick began turning drivers away.

One group of people arrived just early enough that they could find parking and church seating, thanks to the meticulous organizing of Michelle Walsh, who designed a Web page to keep extended family and friends apprised of car pools and arrangements. With the help of Nemeh volunteer Randy Zinn, Michelle had obtained tickets for her first cousin and lifelong best friend Jill Borowy Gadke, as well as Jill's parents and twenty-seven other loved ones. They filled three consecutive pews near the back of the church.

Jill, a thirty-eight-year-old victim of breast cancer, wore a pink ball cap on her bald head. Her parents had brought pillows to pad the wooden pew; even so, she was uncomfortable. Heavy pain medication made Jill drift in and out of consciousness during the six-hour wait for a prayer from Dr. Nemeh. Although she had been told she was terminal, Jill was hoping for a miracle.

At first, the atmosphere in the church was somber. Michelle allowed herself a wry smile as, after having settled into their pews, all twenty-nine of Jill's support group pulled rosaries from their purses and pockets and began to pray. After a while, up in the choir loft, a young woman began singing hymns and inspirational songs. Jill's three pews of supporters stirred, murmuring to one another: *Beautiful . . . unbelievable . . . what a voice . . . I wonder who she is?* Her singing lifted their spirits and stirred the hope that had brought them to this place. Some weeks later, Michelle would learn from Randy Zinn that the singer was the Nemehs' seventeen-year-old daughter, Ashley.

Father Ted, Issam, and Kathy decided there was no point in sticking to the original plan of waiting until after the noon Mass to begin praying over people. Improvising, just before Father Ted began his nine a.m. Mass, Dr. Nemeh stepped out from the sacristy and descended the altar steps to the first row of pews, ready to turn methodically to the task at hand. Al Strnad was watching, and his heart leaped to his throat when a rush of people surged up the center aisle toward the doctor.

Wheelchairs and gurneys rolled forward. It could have been a terrible situation. Ushers reassured everyone their turn would come, and the crowd self-corrected when they recognized they were jeopardizing the safety of the most vulnerable. People returned to their seats, and the dangerous moment passed.

Three hours later Father Ted began his celebration of the final Mass of the day. Simultaneously, Bishop Gries offered Mass over in the activity center. All the while Dr. Nemeh, dressed in black slacks and a black knit sweater, had been moving from person to person, murmuring a quiet prayer over each individual as he extended his hands toward them, sometimes lightly touching his fingers to their head, or pressing his hands gently upon their shoulders, trunk, arms, or legs. The sounds of the priest celebrating Mass were a sound track to his nearly inaudible prayers.

Dr. Nemeh stood before a woman who was holding her five-month-old baby. When he raised his hands to begin his prayer, he recognized something special in the baby's eyes. *Her eyes are shining with spiritual knowledge of the Presence*, he thought. Dr. Nemeh had barely asked the Holy Spirit to come when the baby noticeably relaxed in her mother's arms. He laid his hands on the mother and murmured, "Come Holy Spirit in the name of Jesus Christ. . . ." The woman's eyes fluttered and closed. A volunteer stepped to the mother's side to gather the baby in her arms. Issam continued praying. Within a minute the woman drifted backward into the outstretched arms of a "catcher," a volunteer who lowered her body to the floor and carefully set her head upon the padded wrestling mat beneath her. Both baby and mother rested quietly and peacefully as family members looked on in astonishment.

"What did you do to her?" the baby's father asked Dr. Nemeh, fear in his eyes.

"That's how they go," replied Dr. Nemeh. "And there *is* a healing for the baby."

The doctor moved to the next person.

Dr. Nemeh perceived that this stooped gentleman in his sixties who was afflicted with scoliosis and kyphosis was going to straighten. He reached his hands around the man's shoulders and placed them upon his spine; after a minute or two he moved his hands to the man's shoulders. The man recognized the physical restructuring as it was unfolding. Quietly the man began praising Jesus. Dr. Nemeh felt the spine turn to putty and re-form beneath his hands. The man whispered in the doctor's ear and described what his body was going through. *The Holy Spirit is melting what was broken,* exalted Issam in his mind, *and is rebuilding this gentleman.* The man walked away tall and straight.

D r. Nemeh begins every prayer by requesting the assistance of the Holy Spirit, whom he says is the activator, the one who initiates a series of events that culminates in physical, emotional, and spiritual manifestations. "The Holy Spirit is the mover—the verb—and Jesus is the way to God the Father."

People often ask Dr. Nemeh if he knows who will receive a healing, and he admits he does. "When a healing takes place," he says, "that knowledge is conveyed to me right away. Sometimes I know even before the healing occurs." When pressed to explain how he knows, he answers, "I know because I am able to intuit the love inside people. I sense their spiritual connectedness. When you belong to Christ and you are praying for someone who has that same connectedness, the two of you share similar spirits." Dr. Nemeh says he can recognize this spirit in others, just as old friends can identify each other even after a lifetime apart.

But to say that Dr. Nemeh is limited by the dogma of any one religious denomination is to misread the essence of his mission. Dr. Nemeh says that he has entrusted his faith to an all-powerful but also an all-loving God. He asserts that those who do not accept the Christian Trinity or who are not followers of Jesus are no less entitled to miracles than are Catholics and other Christians. How one worships is a private matter between Father and child. In fact, says Dr. Nemeh, "the people who don't believe in Christ oftentimes will be healed more quickly than anyone." It might be because their hearts are filled with love, or because an amazing manifestation is what it will take for them to recognize the presence of God, he says. Either way, within Dr. Nemeh's medical practice and prayer ministry, examples abound of people who have been made well, but who do not share his religious denomination. Dr. Nemeh maintains steadfast neutrality toward the state of spirituality and religious affiliation of those who come before him. He says, "It is never for me to judge." In his view, he has merely surrendered his arms and hands as tools God will use to help Him obtain something He desires.

And what does God desire? According to Dr. Nemeh, God wants a dynamic, reciprocal relationship with each of His children. He so desires an authentic relationship, one in which He is made part of our lives in the same way we include our best friends, He is willing to prove that He walks among us every day. One proof He offers is the public manifestation of His healing touch. The key to unlocking this dynamic relationship, says Dr. Nemeh, is love.

Making a connection, for Dr. Nemeh, is an important aspect of healing. He believes God resides in each of us, and the Godliness inside sometimes wears the name of Love. "I can feel when there is connectedness made by *either* a lively relationship with God *or* by living in a loving way," says Dr. Nemeh. In explaining this, he points to a biological model. "The body is comprised of many organs. By themselves these organs are useless. Yet when they are connected, each brings its unique contribution to the living being and the organism flourishes." Similarly, St. Paul talks about Jesus as the head of the Body of Christ—that is, the Church. In this tradition, those who have chosen Christ are essential members having equal rank within the whole body. "When you are organs of the same body you are linked to one another. This is why I can feel it when people are open to me. Because I'm merely another one of the parts, as integral in the healthy, robust functioning of the whole as everyone else, I can feel connectedness. And sometimes when people don't think they believe in God, the *love* in their hearts is what provides the connection."

Reverend Channing Smith, rector of St. Andrew's Episcopal Church in Saratoga, California, agrees with Dr. Nemeh about the importance of being connected. Reverend Smith hosted the Nemehs for a series of healing services in Marin County, California, over Thanksgiving weekend in 2008. Reverend Smith blessed people as Dr. Nemeh prayed over them. From this close perspective and from the overwhelming number of healing testimonials shared afterward by his parishioners, Reverend Smith believes that Dr. Nemeh helps to realign people with

God. "Issam brings a reordering," he says. "And that timeless moment of connection with God brings about healings."

Father Dan Schlegel, who has hosted many healing services as pastor of the Church of the Holy Angels in Bainbridge, Ohio, explains from his perspective what happens when Dr. Nemeh prays. "Part of 'miracle' is understanding and experiencing the unconditional love of God. When we do that there is a power and strength that dwells within us and we are able to endure our burdens, whether they are physical, emotional, or spiritual. Issam is a conduit of God's love. By being a vehicle of that love he helps people carry their burdens."

4

Greater Purpose

Tens of thousands of people have experienced astounding physical, emotional, and spiritual changes since Dr. Nemeh opened his acupuncture practice in 1992. Dr. Nemeh accepted that most people waiting for a prayer at Sts. Peter and Paul Church thought these transformations were what he was all about. It is his contention, however, that the healings are not in and of themselves the point.

When cancerous tumors vanish, vision is restored to the blind, and other dramatic changes occur in people after receiving a prayer, Dr. Nemeh's perception of these happenings is a little different from most people's. He sees healings and miracles as "manifestations," by which he means they are demonstrations of God's presence. They are proof that God is closer than we think He is. They are signs that He walks beside us in everything we do. They are also God's hand-delivered invitations to engage in a loving relationship with Him. Dr. Nemeh believes God is willing to provide these displays of His unlimited power because He is seeking our free will decision to love Him.

"God is up to a greater purpose with these manifestations,

whether great or small," says Dr. Nemeh. "The miracles are just to get our attention."

As the contact person representing Father Ted and Sts. Peter and Paul Church, Al Strnad was constantly on the move and was therefore privileged to witness extraordinary moments on the Day of the Ten Thousand. He was there when the first person was called from the activity center over to the church, and he held open the door as this man wheeled the chair in which was strapped his paralyzed son. Walking beside the father as they crossed the campus, Al read in the man's face a mixture of desperation and hope. At first there was only the sound of sidewalk salt crunching beneath their feet. Then the father told Al about the tragedy that had brought him to Sts. Peter and Paul that day. "My son was in a terrible car accident. His back was broken; he should have died. I have driven all the way from Texas because I have faith. I brought my son here just in case it can help." Although Al never again caught sight of this man and his son after they disappeared into the church, Al would always remember the expression on that father's face.

Al happened to be in the church when a woman who could not walk rose from her wheelchair and did what she had been told was impossible. He expected she would look happy or celebratory. He was not so much amazed that she walked as he was touched to see reflected in her face not jubilation, but peacefulness.

During the twenty-two hours he was on-site Al saw thousands of people coming and going. The overwhelming impression that registered for him was hope. "If there was desperation," he said, "it was always cloaked with hope. People didn't come looking for the quick fix, at least not the ones I talked to. They came looking for answers. They were searching for hope.

"And the volunteers were more reinforced in their spirituality than anyone because they witnessed the holiness for many, many hours. The Holy Spirit was permeating the grounds. At the end of the day what remained was the exquisite knowledge that there is an infinite array of gifts out there that can be a pathway to God."

On this day, the atmosphere in the church caused Issam to feel a rush of tangled emotions coming in all at once. He perceived the hope, sadness, and faith coming from these patient people. He looked on every person in the same way, thinking, as he moved from one to the next, *Everyone is a child of God.* Dr. Nemeh says he feels no ethnicity, no cultural belongingness whatsoever, but just the identification that we all belong to God. It is this sense of relatedness that makes him aware of his own humanity in his work. He says, "I am a human being. I recognize the mercy and the love of God. The Holy Spirit is the One who guides and enlightens and purifies us. My job is simply to be an extension of that."

His personal appearance reflects this Everyman identity. He stands five foot ten and perpetually needs to lose a few pounds, a consequence of the double-digit hours he spends at the office as well as his appreciation of good food. He wears his hair combed neatly over the top of his head from a deep part, and it cascades to a small tangle of curls in the back. It's difficult to catch the hazel color behind his eyeglasses. His look is as pleasant and unassuming as that of Winnie the Pooh, his demeanor as gentlemanly as Walter Cronkite's. He would never stand out in a crowd . . . unless, that is, he is praying. Then he becomes unforgettable. When he prays he has a look of being lost in another world.

He is polite, respectful, and gentle while praying, yet he zeroes in on body parts like sonar in a submarine, showing no hesitation or indecision. He knows what he is about here. All the while he is laying his hands on people, an unself-conscious, continuous montage of expressions plays over his face. His eyes may squinch shut or flutter halfway open. He may engage visually with the person he is praying over, or look upward toward the heavens, or gaze into the distance. He may look sad, or intense, or sometimes even happy, but there is always a look of otherworldliness about him. People try to catch what he is saying as he prays, but his voice is a gentle wash of sounds impossible to discern. The cadence of his prayer is as soothing as the rustle of leaves in a summer breeze, and the sequence of his words as impossible to duplicate as the lapping of waves upon the shore.

D r. Nemeh had been praying over people for many hours on the Day of the Ten Thousand when he walked up to a young woman in her twenties and raised his hands. Right away he knew there was cancer. *I see an enormous faith in her,* he thought, and yet, simultaneously, he felt a dark force coming from somewhere on his right. Dr. Nemeh had no way of knowing that the twenty-something woman's father had objected to any talk of taking his cancer-ridden daughter to the healing service. When it became clear his daughter was dying and it was time to speak of last wishes he vowed, "Whatever you want, I will do."

She answered, "Take me to the healing service this week-end."

He did. He was resentful and suspicious but he kept his promise. While standing next to the young lady Dr. Nemeh felt the negative energy emanating from this man, and it pierced their moment. Glancing in the father's direction, Dr. Nemeh asked the girl, "Who is mad at me?"

"That's my dad," she responded.

Dr. Nemeh looked at the man. *I feel a connectedness there and that bodes well,* he thought. He redirected his prayer toward the father, then turned back to the young lady and prayed over her. She got her miracle. In years to come, she and Kathy would cross paths at the local store where the young lady worked. She always gets a little teary-eyed when she sees Kathy. She never fails to give her a big hug and ask about Issam, saying, "How is my favorite doctor? You know, if it weren't for him, I wouldn't be here! Tell him I pray for him all the time, and please give him my best."

Dr. Nemeh often confronts negativity and skepticism in his work. "Family members tell me 'I don't need your prayer—I'm just here with my spouse.' I see through the bitter-ness of caretakers who really wish the sick person would just die. Sometimes the adult child of a geriatric patient is hop-ing the parent will give up because the caregiving burden is so great. They may have been forced to go along with the healing service excursion but their thoughts are transparent to me."

Dr. Nemeh says he can sense when people will not receive the miraculous healings they seek. He says that he prays with just as much intensity nevertheless because he might be proven wrong. He believes that even if there is no healing, the physical journey of the sick is always a spiritual blessing to their souls because, as he explains, "It's all about love, relationship, and surrendering to the will of the Father."

When Dr. Nemeh begins his prayer it is as though he becomes a diagnostician of the body as well as of the spirit. "I can tell if this one will need more prayer and if that one will receive a gradual but complete healing. Oftentimes I am given a message that will help in the completion of the healing. I have, for example, prayed countless times over people sunk in clinical depression. I advise them, 'You will be healed if you surrender everything to God.' Many do focus on that surrender, and I can tell when they have accepted the Spirit's influence. Even if they don't, I continue praying, for there is always the hope they will be able to get to that point in faith where they *can* refocus on belonging to the Body of Christ. Where they *will* accept the Spirit. Some people shove the Spirit away, and when they do I feel a physical push."

Bringing people closer to God gives Issam joy. He is devastated and saddened when people over whom he prays reject God. Still he disciplines himself to remain nonjudgmental. "If I belong to Christ," he reasons, "I have to be truthful. There is nothing that can be hidden. I must have a steady surrender now and forever in order for the connection to be made. There cannot be judging of others. I cannot interpret shortcomings of others in a negative light. That would be evil, and evil does not exist simultaneously with good."

Although Dr. Nemeh was not surprised by the numbers of people who came to Sts. Peter and Paul Church, he was amazed by their patience. As soon as people received their prayers and departed, others took their places, and they waited with the same charity toward others as had those before them. It was as though by common agreement the regular rules of an express-lane society had been suspended. Everyone sacrificed a little of their own personal agendas and by doing so became participants in the greater purpose of the event.

5

The Faces of Faith

It was Pastor Ted Marszal's first Nemeh healing service and he was shocked at what he was witnessing. He had never seen anything like it. He talked of closing the church as early as seven o'clock in the evening, nervous that the crowd would eventually become restless and disgruntled at the lengthy waiting times. He relaxed when he saw that the police and fire chiefs were pleased with how the event was being managed. As he circulated in the church and hallways, he realized people accepted the inevitability of a long wait and were not complaining. Parish volunteers had rallied to support their pastor, and an air of excitement and camaraderie simmered as they busied themselves meeting the needs of the people. He also noted that those who were waiting to have their moment with Dr. Nemeh were using the time to pray, and that was always a good thing. For Father Ted, however, the most compelling reason he changed his mind was what he saw in the faces of the people who had come for a prayer. "Just to see their faces afterward," he said. "Each one was different, but in most cases there was a sense of peace in their expressions. There was a sense of reverence and peacefulness. It was just beautiful." When Issam learned that the priest had abandoned the notion of closing the church early in the evening, he rejoiced. *Ahh,* thought Issam when he heard the good news. *He is able to see that the hand of Jesus is at work.*

While Issam prayed, Kathy decided she should try to help the people waiting outside. She scouted for corners, benches, or pews where she could place them. At one point she opened a heavy church door and saw a face she would never forget. A very old, very tiny woman wearing a babushka and a long black coat stood there, shivering in the cold. Rosary beads dangled from her shaking hands. In a foreign accent, with halting words, she asked, "Please. Please can I come in?"

"Of course," Kathy murmured. The woman's faith took her breath away. "Are you by yourself?" She extended her arm to draw the woman inside and squeezed her into a pew. All day, everywhere she looked, Kathy saw people in need and felt as though she were bailing a boat with a paper cup.

At times throughout the day Kathy prayed alongside Issam, for she, too, has the gift of prayer that comes, she says, from "faith that never doubts." Her style is different from her husband's: she stands to the side as she prays rather than in front of a person. Sometimes, however, people will reach out and pull her in close. Issam is as patient as stone, but Kathy likes to get things done quickly; that is how she has lived her life and it is how she prays her prayers. "It's my ADHD spirit," she says, laughing. Her sunny disposition and mischievous sense of humor make her approachable—but there is no doubt her prayers are powerful. The catchers scramble to keep up when she joins Issam on the prayer line.

Whereas Dr. Nemeh rarely engages in conversation, sometimes Kathy comforts parents as her husband prays over their children. Many parents tell her, "We wish it was us and not our little one." Kathy takes their sorrow to the mother of Jesus. "I always go to Blessed Mother when I pray with these moms and dads. 'Please,' I pray, 'you saw how your son suffered on the Cross. Please don't let this child suffer. Please don't let this mother watch her child suffer.' It gets emotional for me. Sometimes I pray God gives the gift of peace."

Like Issam, Kathy is able to sense who will "fall in the Spirit" and who will not. Being touched by the Holy Spirit is not the same as fainting because the person retains consciousness. Those who have experienced falling in the Spirit say it is the opposite of losing consciousness. They say they feel a heightened awareness that becomes so overwhelming that the body's energy fades and cannot support the person in an upright position. There are biblical precedents, including the description of soldiers falling when Jesus spoke to them in Gethsemane, and Saul of Tarsus falling to the ground when he was on his way to Damascus and Christ appeared to him. People who have been overwhelmed by the Holy Spirit are said to be "resting in the Spirit." At a Nemeh healing service, most people remain in this private, intensely sensory experience for just a few minutes; sometimes, however, people can rest in the Spirit for up to an hour.

When she prays over people Kathy, like Dr. Nemeh, can discern who will reject the prayer out of fear or from a lack of surrender. She is sympathetic to the struggles of these people for she, too, had to surrender to God. "I learned how to give myself over to the Holy Spirit," she says. "Now I ask God to help me, and then I just *know* where to place my hands."

On this Day of the Ten Thousand, she prayed over a

woman who was trembling. "Don't be afraid," she soothed. "Why are you shaking? What are you afraid of? You're only going to touch a little bit of heaven." Then she prayed from her heart that God would reach out and provide what the woman needed.

Later another woman buried her face in Kathy's shoulder and would not let go. She sobbed, "I don't want to die. I don't want to die!" Kathy held her. "Don't be afraid," Kathy said. "Just take a walk with Jesus and talk to him like He's your best friend." When she glanced up, Kathy noticed tears trickling down the face of the catcher who was standing behind the woman.

A pancreatic cancer patient had come with his children, wife, brothers, sisters, nephews, and nieces. They cried and cried. Their love for each other was obvious. The sick man told Kathy, "I found my faith. 'Thy will be done.' That's all I can say. I'll be fine. I just worry about my wife and children." Kathy marveled at his strength.

Just before four o'clock in the afternoon an usher approached and told Kathy about a mother who said that she had been waiting six hours and that her daughter could not hold out much longer. Kathy whispered to Issam, and they made their way to the back of the church where Jill Borowy Gadke, Michelle Walsh's cousin, propped in the pew on now-flattened pillows, was fading fast. Her support group of twenty-nine people filed out of their three pews and gathered right there in the center aisle, forming a circle around Jill, Kathy, and the doctor. They reached out to join hands with one another.

Watching Dr. Nemeh and Kathy place their hands on Jill and pray, and seeing the series of physical reactions and changes washing over Jill's body, was an intensely emotional experience for Michelle. When Jill's features relaxed Michelle rejoiced. Then she saw an expression of relief come over Jill's countenance, and she thanked God.

When the prayer was over and the family turned to gather their coats from the pews, Michelle nearly tripped over something on the ground. Looking down, Michelle was surprised to see her sister-in-law lying on the floor, out cold; when she came to, she confessed, "This powerful, positive thing came from within me and made me collapse!" The experience would inspire a renewal of faith for Michelle's sister-in-law.

Michelle waited with Jill in the vestibule as Jill's father fetched the car. Weak as she was, Jill somehow found the strength to say, "I felt something, Michelle. Something came over me. I'm glad we came."

Early in the afternoon Philip Keller, a morning radio personality known to Clevelanders as WDOK's "Trapper Jack" and a patient of Dr. Nemeh's, now a devoted friend, was handed a bullhorn and led outside. Legally blind, he was unable to see the hundreds of people who were clustered in the courtyard, but Kathy had asked him to reassure everyone that their patience would be rewarded, so he climbed on a bench and announced, "Everyone will get a prayer. Every person will get the prayer you came for."

About twelve hours later, at one in the morning, it occurred to Philip that the surprise for him was not the number of people who had shown up at Sts. Peter and Paul but that for the very first time some went home without having received the prayer that Dr. Nemeh would love to have prayed for them.

6.

Attitude Adjustment

In his capacity as Nemeh emissary in charge of crowd control on the Day of the Ten Thousand, firefighter, part-time police officer, husband, and father of three Lieutenant Patrick Coleman spent an eighteen-hour day in the church parking lot. He noted license plates from many different states and parked a charter bus that had come from Canada. He met people who had traveled from Japan to be prayed over by Dr. Nemeh. Throughout the long, cold day, he reflected on how two years earlier Dr. Nemeh's prayer had miraculously changed his life for the better.

In June 2003 Patrick's mother, Carolyne Coleman, heard about a Dr. Nemeh healing service to be held at St. Mary of the Assumption Chapel on the campus of St. Ignatius High School, and she urged her son to attend. Diagnosed with celiac sprue, a genetic chronic disease of the digestive tract for which the only known treatment is complete avoidance of gluten in the diet, Patrick was very sick. He had lost weight and had become uncharacteristically lackluster about life, and Carolyne was worried.

"No way," he snapped.

"But Patrick. It's Father's Day. The service starts with Mass; we'll all go with you. Do it for your father and because you are a father."

"Mom, you're a travel agent for guilt trips."

On Father's Day 2003 Patrick put on a blue striped shirt, tucked it into a pair of khakis, and arrived at St. Mary of the Assumption Chapel in time for Mass. Skeptical though he was, he was truly sick of being sick. When it was his turn for a prayer, Patrick tried to listen to what Dr. Nemeh was saying but could not catch any particular words.

Absolutely nothing happened.

That would have been the end of it except that as Patrick was leaving the chapel Kathy spotted him talking to her aunt, Dolores Maroon, a lady Patrick had known from his childhood. Later, when Issam told Kathy that the man in the blue striped shirt could have a healing if he returned for another prayer, Kathy knew how to track down this nameless man. Three days later Carolyne called Patrick to convey Kathy Nemeh's request that he call her.

Patrick hung up from his mother and punched in Kathy's phone number. "Hi, my name is Patrick Coleman. I'm told you wanted me to call you."

"Oh, hello, Patrick. Were you wearing a blue striped shirt when you came to St. Mary's?"

"Yes."

"Dr. Nemeh felt you resisting and would like you to come back. You don't have to, but he would like you to." The hair on the back of Patrick's neck stood straight up.

Kathy informed him of the dates of the next healing services and they hung up.

Patrick attended the August healing service accompanied

by his wife, Karen, his parents, John and Carolyne, and his fire-fighter brother, John. This time when Dr. Nemeh prayed over him, Patrick says, he closed his eyes and "gave it up to God." Dr. Nemeh put his hand on Patrick's abdomen and the moment he did so Patrick felt a tremendous spreading warmth. He tried to open his eyes but could not. At that point Patrick said a silent prayer: "Lord, I am not worthy, but only say the word and I shall be healed." Patrick's legs buckled and he collapsed into the pew right behind him. His family watched, concerned, as his breathing changed to shallow, quick panting. Patrick experienced a sensation of someone holding his head back, and he struggled to break free of the restraint.

After some time Patrick opened his eyes. He looked for the doctor but saw that Dr. Nemeh had moved on down the prayer line. Wobbly-kneed, he staggered to a pew near the back of the chapel. His family slid in beside him. He rested his elbows on his knees, held his head in his hands, and tried to collect himself. Worried, Karen touched him on the arm and asked, "Are you all right?"

"Yeah, sure. I'm fine."

As a matter of fact, he realized, he did feel remarkably better. Physically, he felt really great. That was weird in and of itself.

"What the heck just happened?" he muttered. "Who was holding my head back?"

His parents, brother, and wife looked at one another, too startled to respond. Finally, his brother spoke up. "No one was holding your head back."

"Bull!" Patrick exclaimed.

"*Pat*rick!" hissed his mother. "You are in *church!*"

"*Some*body was holding my head down!"

They just stared at him.

"Nobody was holding my head down?" he asked. *How could that be?* He lapsed into stony silence, went into a deeply personal zone, and everyone else just faded away.

I was not afraid, he thought. *I asked for something. I asked to be healed. Then I got an invasion of my body—but still I was not afraid. Why not?* Then he realized: *The Holy Spirit came into me. I felt the Holy Spirit's presence inside my soul. For the first time, I can actually feel my soul. I can feel all the way into my soul.* Patrick thought it was a tremendous thing, an astounding thing, to be introduced to the core of one's essence. It was as though he had been held in the palm of God's healing hand. It was unforgettable.

Patrick came away from that second encounter with Dr. Nemeh with a new appreciation that there is only the sheerest partition between earth and heaven. "I felt touched by heaven," he says. "Heaven is right here. What a cool thing to know that the angels are close at hand, here to warn and help us. What a supercool thing that the Holy Spirit could be so close, close enough to heal a sick firefighter with a lousy attitude."

After leaving the service, Patrick decided to test the waters right away. Across the street from the St. Ignatius campus is a Wendy's restaurant. He steered his blue conversion van into the drive-thru line. Karen was worried. "Are you sure you want to do this?" she asked. He answered, "Why not?" The next day he ate pizza, a delicacy he had not enjoyed since his diagnosis. It tasted fabulous. And . . . there was no adverse reaction.

Patrick revisited the medical community to have his hunch validated. His insurance covered the endoscopy, biopsies, and all the other tests, all of which came back negative. He read the follow-up letter to his folks over the phone: " 'We have no explanation why, blah blah blah . . . however, we recommend you continue on the gluten-free diet.' " He chuckled. "No way!"

Patrick's family planned to attend the next healing service, this time to give thanks for Patrick's healing. When he arrived at St. Mary of the Assumption Chapel, Patrick searched the crowd for Kathy. Finding her, he approached and asked if he could thank the doctor. "Of course," she answered, and began leading him to her husband. As they walked, she asked if Patrick would mind saying a few words about his healing. Part of him didn't want to do it. He wasn't the type to go public with his innermost feelings. He wrestled with himself. *How can I not? That's the least I can do for these people,* he thought. With some trepidation he agreed.

Kathy and Patrick found Issam alone, leaning against a wall.

"Hello, Dr. Nemeh," Patrick said, extending his hand. "I just want to thank you from the bottom of my heart."

The doctor smiled. "Don't thank me," he replied. "Thank God."

After Mass, Patrick stepped to the microphone and told his story. The crowd responded with a warm round of applause.

Patrick and Karen decided to keep coming to subsequent services together, and at the next one Patrick was stopped by a woman just as they were entering St. Mary of the Assumption Chapel, and she asked, "Are you the fireman who was here last time?"

Patrick nodded. "Yes, that's me." He shook her hand and introduced himself.

"I want to thank you." At this point the lady broke down crying. Through her tears she continued. "I came to the last healing service with stage IV ovarian cancer. I was going to leave right after Mass because I was very skeptical. But you stepped up to the microphone and I thought, *Oh, I may as well listen to what he has to say.* I heard your story and then decided to stay for a prayer from the doctor. And now . . . now my cancer is *gone!*" This lady taught Patrick you should never keep God-given gifts to yourself.

Eighteen months later, in February 2005, Cleveland's WEWS News Channel 5 aired *Healing Miracles*, the eleven-part series in which Ted Henry reported on "an unprecedented number of faith healings happening right here in Cleveland, Ohio." Patrick was watching the broadcast one night when Henry announced that a service would be held at Sts. Peter and Paul in just a few weeks, and ticket information was displayed on a banner. It occurred to the public servant in Patrick that these folks might need some help. He scrounged around for Kathy's phone number, called, and offered his assistance.

Kathy accepted. "Would you mind handling crowd control? We have a service coming up on March 13 at Sts. Peter and Paul."

"I know about it."

"There will be a meeting at the rectory. Can you come?"

"Sure," he answered. After they hung up, Patrick reflected how he had never fully appreciated the gift of health until it had been taken away, and how being sick had inspired in him a new sense of compassion for those who were ill and infirm.

He felt good about having volunteered. It was a small thing he could do for Dr. Nemeh, after the doctor had sought out Patrick and invited him to return for the prayer that would deliver his healing. Even more than that, Patrick viewed his volunteering as a way of giving back to God, who, just like Dr. Nemeh, had cared enough to pursue him until he had been blessed with the miracle God was hoping he would accept.

❧

7

Grace Moments

Issam continued praying throughout the day at Sts. Peter and Paul, sidestepping from person to person, unaware of anything outside his quiet zone. At around five that evening Father Ted, Issam, Kathy, and the Nemeh volunteers walked through the breezeway to the rectory for dinner. The food Kathy had cooked and Issam had unloaded from their car early that morning was set out on long tables. There were birthday cakes for Father Ted and Philip Keller, but everyone hurried through dinner and dessert so they could get back to the church and resume the prayers.

Father Ted approached Issam and Kathy at around eight o'clock. Something was telling him that he and Dr. Nemeh should make an appearance over in the activity center. "I feel like I'm being led there . . . led by God," he told the Nemehs. Dr. Nemeh suspended his prayers in the church and he followed Father Ted across the cold courtyard over to the activity center.

Father Ted opened the heavy door, stepped inside, then halted, overwhelmed by the sight of more than five hundred silent people jammed into the space. Many were fingering rosaries. Others were sitting with their hands folded, some praying, some lost in thought. The utter silence of their vigil took his breath away. Only after the priest had mastered his emotions was he able to move forward, making way for Issam, Kathy, and Sister Monica to wade, single file, into the crowd. A sea of people parted to make way for them.

People reached out to touch Dr. Nemeh as he walked by. Young ones were lifted and passed to the doctor through the hands of strangers. As Issam wandered through the space the crowd accommodated him in silence.

Father Ted's heart swelled. He would always remember walking through the sea of sick and hurting people. It was what he called a perfect grace moment.

Dr. Nemeh would never forget these moments either, but for different reasons. In the seven hours since Philip promised that everyone would receive a prayer, it had become apparent to Dr. Nemeh that this promise could not be kept. "I was stricken with unbearable grief because I recognized the need of so many," he recalled of his team's slow procession through this room. "When they reached out to touch me, I was reduced to tears. At that moment I renewed my offering. *I renew it more*, I told God. *I renew my promise to offer my life to You even more.* Walking through that place was one of the saddest things I have ever done. I was thinking, *I can feel the love of Jesus for these people. His love is so vivid! So many faces, none of whom would receive a prayer! So many souls! So many, many lost opportunities!* I felt like a failure."

Kathy spotted a woman who was watching them with eyes that called to her. She and Issam brushed past Tricia Kaman, a portrait artist who had spent her entire career studying people so that she could capture their essence in her art.

"When I saw them walk in the room," Tricia recalled, "I

gasped. They were a stunning couple. On his face I saw compassion. On her face I saw love. As they moved closer to me I saw in this couple a mature spirituality, a compelling, charismatic presence, and an unforgettable quality of *being*."

The Nemehs made this brief visit because Father Ted said he was called to go there. Neither Dr. Nemeh nor Kathy prayed a healing prayer over anyone; they didn't see how they could pray over two, three, or ten when five hundred were waiting with such patience. If there was a purpose to this cameo appearance, perhaps it was to demonstrate to the faithful, such as Tricia, that a prayer from this man who wore compassion so plainly on his face would be worth the wait. Maybe the purpose was to remind Issam of the work that lay ahead for him. Father Ted was thinking that what he called a perfect grace moment held within it a hint of the Bible being reenacted.

Father Ted remembered the eight hundred people who were waiting for their prayers over in the church, and turned toward the exit. Dr. Nemeh, Kathy, and Sister Monica followed. As quickly as they had arrived, they were gone.

Tricia tried to return to her prayers but was distracted by the memory of their faces. Their eyes were emblazoned in her mind.

Even though he was concerned for all the people who were waiting, Father Ted made the decision that he could not permit the prayers to continue all night. He recognized that this day was a unique and extraordinary moment in time but he felt a sense of duty to clear the grounds and ready the school for the teachers and children. Also, his parish volunteers were exhausted. Sometime before midnight he assumed the unpleasant duty of announcing to those waiting in the activity center, "Those presently in the church will be the last group to receive a prayer from Doctor Nemeh. Everyone else must go home."

When the hope of praying for everyone had begun to unravel, Kathy pondered what could be done. In a moment she could only credit to Divine Intervention, she knew. She telephoned Father Thomas L. Weber, pastor of St. Bernadette's in Westlake. She explained the situation. "Kathy, yes, of course you can have St. Bernadette's," he said. "You can have our church for as long as you need." Two new healing services were scheduled: one for Monday, March 14 and another for Saturday, March 19. It then became Patrick's job to hand out numbered cards so the team could estimate how many people might come to St. Bernadette's. At first he distributed one per person, but when he began to run low on cards he wrote a note on the back, specifying how many in a group or family could be admitted with this one card.

Rain checks for prayers.

Seat belt fastened and heat blasting on high, Tricia set out just after midnight for the long ride from Garfield Heights to her home in Chagrin Falls. She called her husband and told him that seeing the Nemehs had made her more determined than ever, and that on Saturday, March 19, she would go to St. Bernadette's and would wait as long as it took for her moment with the doctor.

At around two in the morning Patrick Coleman surveyed the parking lot, serene for the first time since he had arrived at eight on Sunday morning. The day had been cold but heartwarming; exhausting but exhilarating; surreal but inspiring. He felt confident that he could leave his post long enough to have a snack and a drink, so he walked over to the rectory.

Patrick was walking through the quiet parking lot toward the rectory when Philip Keller also had a thought of foraging for something to eat. Philip asked a volunteer to lead him from the church over to the priest's kitchen. Quite by accident, then, Patrick and Philip found themselves standing side by side in the shadows of the rectory's Cleaver-esque kitchen. There they shared what Philip calls "the Wow Moment": a moment in which they tasted and savored the Wow-ness of what they had witnessed. They marveled over Dr. Nemeh's impeccable patience, and how he was completely unaware of time as he prayed over person after person. They admired Kathy and her indomitable energy. They were amazed at the people, so hopeful, patient, and willing to cooperate with whatever needed to be done. Patrick and Philip sunk into a moment of timelessness in this hushed corner.

This was the beginning of a new era for the Nemeh ministry, not just because Ted Henry's televised coverage had blown wide open the previously well-kept secret of Dr. Nemeh's quiet practice and dignified healing services, but also because Patrick would become the event organizer for the Nemehs. He would perform a multitude of tasks for twenty-four healing events over the next two and a half years, and his organizational efforts would create a viable structure for Dr. Nemeh's public prayer ministry.

Every Nemeh healing service concludes with an opportunity for the volunteers to receive their own prayers from the doctor and his wife. At two thirty in the morning, when the extraordinary day at Sts. Peter and Paul was about to end, Father Ted hovered close as his parish volunteers lined up for their prayers. They had watched thousands come and go; at last it was their turn to feel the doctor's hands on them. Some were in tears. Al Strnad, who had worked so hard for his parish this day, has chronic obstructive pulmonary disease (COPD). He was impressed when the doctor and Kathy, without having been told of his condition, placed their hands directly over the area where he was having the most difficulty breathing.

Taking it all in, Father Ted said he experienced "the second perfect grace moment of the day. It was a moment of bonding within the inner group who had made this thing work, and there was a real sense of the presence of God and His healing touch in their midst."

The last of the volunteers congregated, reluctant to see this special moment end. Though they were physically tired, their spirits were elated, and everyone was quiet but happy. Kathy and Issam felt energized. In the frosty early morning air, Patrick and Al helped them load empty serving platters and bowls into the trunk of their car. Al stayed behind to jot some thank-you notes and write up a report of the day, finishing at four in the morning.

Kathy and Issam drove Philip to his house, then headed for home. Issam worried about those who had come in search of a miracle but had left without receiving a prayer. He took a brief nap and then reported for his usual day at the office.

Part Two

ANSWER
"THE CALL"

~

8

The Doctor Is In

For fifteen years, Dr. Nemeh's office day typically began as early as nine o'clock and rarely ended before the early-morning hours of the following day. However, in 2009 Kathy assumed the position of appointment secretary and began scheduling fewer patients each day. For the first time in his career, Dr. Nemeh now sees his last patients sometime before midnight.

He spends six days a week in a three-room suite located in a Rocky River office building a mile and a half from home. Once there, the doctor never leaves, so for years Kathy has cooked lunch and dinner for Issam and secretaries Carmie Pruchnicki and Tia Boukis. The furnishings are modest but neat and tidy. Kathy makes certain the waiting room has a tray of cookies or an assortment of candy and pretzels set out in bowls for patients and their families. Religious paintings and icons decorate the walls and adorn the tabletops, all of them given by patients in gratitude for Dr. Nemeh's care.

Patients are charged for acupuncture treatments, of course, since this is the doctor's means of making a living. Most medical insurance carriers do not include acupuncture as a covered treatment, so the full burden of payment is usually on the patient. Some carriers offer a "wellness benefit" and others an acupuncture rider, but these policies are uncommon.

Acupuncture, an ancient pain-management technique that originated in China, is more widespread throughout Asia than it is in the United States. In Japan, a recent study of two thousand randomly selected subjects showed roughly 25 percent of the population will avail themselves of acupuncture in their lifetime. By comparison, in the United States roughly 10 percent of the population will seek treatment from one of approximately seventeen thousand acupuncture practitioners in their lifetime. It is estimated that more than 20 million Americans, or, approximately one in ten adults, have received acupuncture treatments.

In the 1960s, researchers Ronald Melzack, Ph.D., and Patrick Wall, M.D., presented a paper in which they detailed the pathway of pain. They argued that pain is conveyed to the brain via the spinal column by means of small, slow-moving cells known as type C nerve fibers. There are also large and fast-moving cells called A-beta fibers that inhibit pain. Melzack and Wall theorized that if the A-beta fibers were to be stimulated, they should be able to override the perceived pain sensation that comes from the C fibers, inhibiting the transmission of pain messages to the brain. They proposed the Gate Theory, which states that by stimulating A-beta nerve fibers, a gating mechanism can be triggered, closing off the pathway of pain signals to the brain. Their second collaborative work, "Pain Mechanisms: A New Theory," was published in the November 1965 issue of *Science*. In this paper they explained how the perception and redirection of the neuronal pathways of pain can be manipulated. This theory of pain management is the basis of acupuncture.

At Dr. Nemeh's office sometimes people are treated with prayer only. For instance, Sue Sidun is one of the patients who have sought the doctor's prayers to avoid surgery and invasive medical procedures. Eighty-five-year-old Sue stopped by one evening in September 2009 with her friend Sister Elizabeth Anne of the Sisters of the Incarnate Word and Blessed Sacrament, ostensibly for a friendly visit. When the doctor emerged from the treatment room, having finished with a patient, and saw the two women sitting in the waiting room, he grinned and immediately began chatting with them. After a few minutes Sue confessed that there was a specific purpose to her visit.

"Doctor, remember those five kidney stones you prayed over? Well, the X-rays showed only four of them disappeared. Would you mind praying over the last one?"

Dr. Nemeh chuckled, walked over to where Sue was seated, placed his hands on her abdomen, and bowed his head in prayer. When the prayer was over, Sue said, "I just know that last stone will disappear!" Sue and Sister Elizabeth Anne left the office happy as could be and had dinner at the Arby's next door.

Patient profiles are diverse. Many have been with the doctor for years; others come to see him only once or twice and there is no need for further treatment. Oftentimes patients incorporate visits to Dr. Nemeh as part of their regular, preventive health care routine. Others discover him only because a medical crisis has disrupted their lives or the life of someone they love. Sometimes after receiving a healing patients choose Dr. Nemeh as their first line of defense when subsequent health issues come up.

It is probably true that a majority of patients has reached the point of desperation by the time they seek treatment from Dr. Nemeh. Of these, some go on to live healthy, full lives.

Many others do not experience a physical healing but report they received inner strength from the treatment and from Dr. Nemeh's counsel. Often these patients describe an illness that is considerably less painful.

Just as there are different types of patients, there are different types of healings: the gradual one that seems to suggest there is a specific growth journey in store for the patient; the teaser that comes and goes; the healing that is refused; and the instantaneous cure that is sensed in a matter of moments. Kathy calls this quick healing of tough problems a "Holy Bingo."

Blue-eyed, blond-haired twins Linda and Laura Seber are licensed physical therapists and lifelong best friends. They arrived at Dr. Nemeh's office on Tuesday, May 28, 2002, utterly discouraged. Linda had sustained life-altering face, neck, thigh, and jaw injuries in a bicycle accident on July 29, 2001. She had seen one vascular surgeon, two neurologists, two orthopedic physicians, a massage therapist, and two chiropractors. One day Linda broke down sobbing at the apartment the twins share. "Nobody can help me," she wailed. Indeed, after all the specialists she had consulted Linda had regained only a small measure of strength in her shoulders and a mere thirty degrees' range of motion in one arm. "I'm going to be this way the rest of my life!" she said.

Laura consoled her. "There is a reason and purpose for everything," she said. "You have to put your faith and trust in God and He will see you through."

At work one week later Laura heard about a local doctor

who might be able to help her sister. A coworker told Laura her back pain had been successfully treated by Dr. Nemeh. After nine months of appointments with specialists who were not able to alleviate Linda's pain or restore her former level of fitness and mobility, the twins were excited to hear about a new opportunity. Maybe this new doctor would be able to help Linda.

Recalling the day of her first appointment, Linda says that as soon as she entered Dr. Nemeh's treatment room and settled into the treatment chair, she felt a sensation of peace descending upon her. Laura joined her sister during the session. As Dr. Nemeh began his work, starting at Linda's feet, he diagnosed a hematoma with muscle atrophy, the result of an old track injury, and told Linda it would be healed. He continued scanning and probing, working his way up from the lower extremities to her trunk.

Getting up from his wheeled stool and moving behind the head of the treatment chair, Dr. Nemeh stood at Linda's shoulders, behind her, so that she could not see him, but Laura could. He was no longer administering acupuncture probes. It appeared to Laura that the doctor was praying. Laura watched as Dr. Nemeh raised one arm, like a symphony orchestra conductor cueing a section. As he did so, Linda's injured arm followed the same arc. Laura was then astounded to see her sister's arm being raised higher and higher—far beyond the thirty degrees' range of motion previously measured as her best. At this point Dr. Nemeh asked Linda, "Do you believe in angels?"

"I do, with all my heart," she responded.

"They're raising your arm right now," he said. "You are going to be healed."

When Linda Seber's session was concluded, she stood up from the chair and was able to raise both her arms in ways she had not been able to since the bicycle accident. Linda and Laura left Dr. Nemeh's office so overjoyed over Linda's instantaneous healing that they drove straight to their parents' home in Elyria to share the news. Linda told her mother and father, "I want to shout it from the mountaintops: God healed me!"

Years later, when she talks about the healing, Linda's face becomes animated and her eyes sparkle with happiness as she describes what it was like to be restored to her previous, pre-injury state of fitness. "No more specialists! No more physical-, ortho-, neuro-, and massotherapy! I became fully functioning and could do everything without pain and without restriction. I was *healed*!"

The healing brought great joy to the twins on a personal as well as a professional level. Each believes Dr. Nemeh is a living saint and a true instrument of the Lord. "Dr. Nemeh reminded us that God is the true healer," says Linda, as Laura nods in agreement. "He has helped us in our careers by giving us a different mind-set. When we are at work we ask God to help us help our patients, and then we praise God for helping us to help others."

PRAYER OF THE STUPID SERVANT

Oh God, make it so clear that even I, fool that I am, could not screw it up.

—Randy Zinn

Randy Zinn is a musician and president of a computer service company. His experience with Dr. Nemeh is a good example of an instantaneous healing. One late summer day Randy made a house call at Philip Keller's residence to work on the family computer. As he worked, Randy involuntarily emitted expressions of discomfort. Philip took note that Randy was in pain. He asked Randy what was wrong, and Randy explained, "It's my neck. I went to a chiropractor and in the course of his 'treatment' he ruptured a disc. Now I can't turn my head. Hurts like heck."

When Philip asked Randy what he was going to do about the pain, Randy told him he was scheduled for a surgical procedure on September 17 in the course of which the back of his neck would be sliced from side to side. "They're going to make me into a human Pez dispenser," he joked. There would be a lengthy recuperative period, and his doctors' tentative prognosis was that after six to twelve weeks he *might* be able to turn his head.

Philip hesitated, then asked Randy if he prayed, and when the response was an unqualified affirmative, he handed Randy one of Dr. Nemeh's business cards and encouraged him to give the office a call.

When Randy got home he told his wife, Patty, what had happened. "He gave me this," Randy said, and handed her the card.

Patty bolted down the basement steps, calling out, "I'll be right back!" She reappeared with two identical cards, one in each hand. Randy's card had just multiplied.

"Look. Dr. Debbie gave me one of these cards about three years ago when I took one of the kids in for a checkup." Dr. Debbie Ghazoul-Mills, a pediatrician, is Kathy Nemeh's sister.

"We were talking about you and she told me, 'When all else fails, give this guy a call.' I keep trying to throw it away and I can't." The two stared at each other. They knew a sign when they saw one.

Randy scheduled a Saturday morning appointment with Dr. Nemeh. He carried with him all his medical records and copies of his MRIs. Dr. Nemeh greeted Randy by asking, pleasantly, "Why are you here?"

"I have a ruptured disc in my neck. Philip Keller recommended I should see you. Then, coincidentally, my wife had your card as well. It just sort of all added up to *I need to be here*."

The doctor smiled.

"Would you like to see my records? The MRIs?" Randy asked.

"Do you believe in God?"

"I believe in a God who puts the grass on the ground, allows birds to fly, and breathes breath into His servants on this earth," Randy said. "I believe in One who has no limitations and whose word can heal anything. There is nothing He cannot do."

"Well, then, this won't take very long."

Throughout the course of Randy's acupuncture treatment, Dr. Nemeh at times spoke so softly that Randy could not catch what he was saying. Randy realized the doctor was praying. He figured he might as well join Dr. Nemeh in prayer so he shut his eyes and, like toddlers engaged in parallel play, the two men prayed. Perhaps ten minutes passed in this way.

Dr. Nemeh asked, "How do you feel?"

Randy opened his mouth to answer and heard a snap in the back of his neck. He paused in stunned silence. Both men knew what had just happened.

"Thank you," Randy said.

"Don't thank me. Thank the Almighty One."

Randy started to get up from the chair, but Dr. Nemeh stopped him, asking, "Where are you going?"

Confused, Randy stammered, "Well, I was going to go home. I mean, I was just healed. Why do you ask? What do you mean?"

Dr. Nemeh explained, "You still have no feeling in your right thumb, right index finger, and the left side of your middle finger. We are not finished here."

Randy was blown away. How did Dr. Nemeh know these things? Randy hadn't mentioned a word about these other problems to anyone. He hadn't recorded them on the intake questionnaire he had filled out when he arrived for his appointment. There was no way for the doctor to have known about them.

Randy began to shiver.

"What's wrong?" Dr. Nemeh asked.

"I'm freezing." An Atlanta native, Randy always felt chilled in the Cleveland climate. He had learned long ago that he should overdress; on this day in early September he was wearing a wool sweater. Still, he felt very, very cold.

Dr. Nemeh then stood beside Randy, bowed his head over him, laid his hands on his chest, and prayed.

Randy got so hot he felt nauseous. "What was *that*?" Randy exclaimed.

"Your metabolism was just adjusted. How's your finger? Thumb? Other finger? Can you feel them?"

"Yes, I can feel them now. The numbness is totally gone."

"We're not quite done yet."

"Look, I feel bad. I've been in here a long time," Randy said. "There are other people waiting to see you out there."

"It's okay," the doctor assured him. "They can wait a few minutes more. Besides, I will give them all the time they need."

Randy wasn't sure what else Dr. Nemeh was praying for, but after a while the checklist must have been completed because the doctor rose from his swivel stool, smiled at Randy, and left without saying a word.

Issam walked into the office where Kathy was working at the desk and gave her an almost imperceptible nod.

She felt a surge of happiness. *Another Holy Bingo!*

It was as though the disc in Randy's neck had never ruptured. The pain vaporized. Randy canceled his surgery.

9.

⚭

Healings on Hold

Word seems to have gotten around that Dr. Nemeh has a tendency to spontaneously give prayer or treatment to the friends and relatives who come along with his patient. Part of the explanation for this unusual office procedure is the doctor's generous nature. But also Dr. Nemeh is unable to refuse the Holy Spirit's pull to pray over someone who is revealed to him as being in need of, and open to, prayer. While he almost never approaches someone first—he waits to be invited in—he is able to discern which people are silently begging to be noticed. Carloads of family and friends often accompany the patient to the appointment, hoping to meet the doctor. Nearly every day someone receives spontaneous prayer from the doctor.

Very often people will receive a healing just because they are in the room during the treatment of the patient. Sue Sidun came to the doctor on October 3, 2005, with a very large cancerous tumor growing on her ovary. Dr. Nemeh treated her, told her she would be fine, and, indeed, when her surgeon removed the mass, tests proved the tumor to be benign. As if that were not amazing enough, during that same appointment Sister Elizabeth Anne, who had been sitting in the room during Sue's treatment, also received a healing. For forty years Sister had worn eyeglasses, but by the time Sue's acupuncture treatment was completed, Sister could see without her glasses. To this day she does not need to wear corrective lenses.

Some healings are manifested, as if they are invitations to come closer to God, but soon disappear. During his second appointment with the doctor, Hank Panek's fiancée, Pat, received a healing as she sat in the treatment room, but after three days it vanished.

Hank had first heard of the doctor from a coworker who consulted Dr. Nemeh and came away very impressed; on the strength of her recommendation, Hank made an appointment for a health concern that he would prefer to keep private. But when he arrived at the office he began to question whether he really belonged there. He felt guilty, thinking he was infringing on time needed by patients who were desperately ill. Thus his first question to Dr. Nemeh was, "Should I even be here?" Dr. Nemeh just smiled and nodded yes.

Hank returned the next week for a follow-up treatment. He and his fiancée were in the midst of making final arrangements for their upcoming wedding, and there was some time to kill between picking up their marriage license and dinner, so she joined Hank in the treatment room. Dr. Nemeh's back was to her as he worked on Hank.

Partway through the session Pat stood up. Hank thought she was going to leave the room to take a walk but she was only stretching. Without a word, Dr. Nemeh swung around on his swivel stool and extended his hands toward her. Both Hank and Pat realized he was directing a prayer toward her.

Dr. Nemeh had just met Pat for the first time. He did not

know that Pat had experienced deficit hearing and poor vision since childhood. As he prayed, Pat saw the frames around the religious icons begin to radiate with a shimmering, golden aura. By the time Dr. Nemeh was finished praying Pat was able to read the fine print inside the prayers hanging on the walls. Her hearing improved, too. When she was once again seated in her chair, and with her "bad side" to the doctor, she could not help exclaiming, "I can hear you!"

"I know," Dr. Nemeh replied, and he continued working on Hank.

"No, I can *really* hear you."

"I know."

Dr. Nemeh finished Hank's treatment and the couple departed. Years later whenever Pat retold the story of meeting Dr. Nemeh, she emphasized that what amazed her most was the golden glowing frames around the icons. But Pat's healing lasted only three days.

Hank explains, "Pat is a human resource manager for a huge grocery store chain. Her job is very demanding and leaves her with precious little free time, and that time is spent cleaning, shopping, and doing laundry." Hank felt strongly that if only Pat would make the time to return to Dr. Nemeh as a patient, the improvement in her hearing and sight would become permanent. He urged her to make this a top priority. He was mystified when she chose not to.

Dr. Nemeh believes that "people refuse God's healing for many different personal reasons. It can be that they need to have an internal healing of an emotional wound, anger, bitterness, or sometimes they just need to be able to forgive. Sometimes they have become frightened of all the ways their lives will change with the healing. I can feel them pushing it away—it is there for the asking, but still they push it away. Sometimes they are just not ready."

Countless examples abound of this dynamic of "not being ready." Philip Keller shares his own story at healing services. He tells about the night when full vision was restored to him for one full minute. The same thing happened again once during the daytime. It took him months of weekly visits with the doctor, he says, to understand that a precise purpose will be served when God heals his vision. Until then, Philip remains a devoted disciple of the doctor, and waits.

Tricia Kaman, the portrait artist who had come to Sts. Peter and Paul on March 13, 2005, would become one of the doctor's patients, too, but she was frustrated for many months by partial healings of her shoulder. In the course of repeated visits she experienced a precious healing from a deep wound. As a child she had never been allowed to cry, but one day in the doctor's office she received the gift of tears. Her shoulder healing followed soon after.

In Dr. Nemeh's private practice and public ministry he sees that personal histories and human emotions can get in the way of healings that beckon. It's as though the debris of life sometimes prevents people from accessing what is theirs for the taking. And even if the miracles fail to occur for his patients, that does not mean they are unavailable. Dr. Nemeh advises that the proper mind-set—the correct approach to God—will make these changes happen. It is as if these healings are placed on layaway. They are being held, in our names, with infinite patience by the One who waits for us to claim them.

⚬

God Is the Healer Here

Dr. Nemeh has never considered himself an alternative healing practitioner but, rather, one who practices within mainstream medicine. Media coverage typically headlines him as a "faith healer." Even if the context and connotation are intended to be positive, Issam is unhappy with that label. He objects because the term is misleading. His faith does not heal. It makes him available to be used as a conduit of healing if that is God's intention.

One Saturday night Issam came home from the office feeling restless. "Kathy, where can I go?" he asked.

"The only place open at this hour is Walmart, Issam," she responded.

Issam considered this. "I suppose I could go to Walmart. I'll see if they have any of those natural mints I like. I just ran out of them."

"Take Wadi with you. He'd love to keep you company."

Wadi, the namesake of Issam's father and the youngest of their four children, hopped up from the couch, and father and son drove off in the dark of night to prowl the fluorescent whiteout of the local Walmart. While they were browsing, a man approached and asked the question that makes Issam cringe: "Aren't you the faith healer?"

Issam shook his head and smiled pleasantly. "No, I am not."

"You sure do look like him," the man said. He started to walk away but turned and once again asked, "You're really not that faith healer?"

"No, I am not."

"You look *exactly* like him."

When Issam came home he told Kathy about the encounter. "Issam!" she said, scolding.

"Ah, but if the man had asked, 'Are you Dr. Nemeh?' I would have told him, 'Yes, I am.'"

The next morning the Nemehs were at St. Barnabas Anglican Church in Bay Village for a healing service. As fate would have it, the man who had approached Issam at Walmart the night before was one of the first in line for a prayer. Issam just smiled at him and prayed. The man was later overheard exclaiming, "That *is* the man I saw in Walmart last night! I *knew* it was him!"

For Issam, the error in nomenclature is huge. "God, and *only* God, heals." he says. Thousands have tried to convey gratitude to him for their healings but he will not allow it.

If, then, he is not a faith healer, who is he?

He insists there is nothing special about him except that he has been given the gift of faith. "When I approach someone, I have *no doubt* God can and will deliver a healing. There are no limitations to the Almighty One. It is we who put limitations on Him."

Though he maintains he is just another person living his faith, there are those who disagree. When the inimitable Sister Monica Marie Navin tells the story of the miracle that launched Issam's public prayer ministry, she says she thinks he is a saint. She speaks of the "healing powers that Jesus gave Dr. Nemeh" and proclaims in her no-nonsense Irish brogue, "I just love Dr. Nemeh—his goodness, spirituality, humility, gentleness, prayerfulness, and kindness."

News Channel 5 received an avalanche of more than four thousand letters in response to Ted Henry's February 2005 series. In the two months following that series, more than thirty thousand individuals sought prayer from Dr. Nemeh at his public healing events.

Two years later, in mid-February 2007, WKYC-TV 3's morning talk show, *Good Company*, focused on Dr. Nemeh for an entire week in a series called "Prayers of the Heart." The station's Web site registered 37,000 hits in February as compared with the more typical 4,000 hits the previous month.

In North Canton, pediatrician Dr. Gregory Spohn was unable to open his office on Valentine's Day that year due to a blizzard that had made roads impassable. Only because he was forced to stay home was Dr. Spohn able to catch that morning's "Prayers of the Heart" segment. When he watched Dr. Nemeh's interview, something clicked, and he knew he wanted to take his wife, Julie, to see Dr. Nemeh.

Julie had suffered extensive neurological damage from a freak accident in a restaurant thirteen years earlier. Eating, walking, talking, and thinking were daily challenges that had completely altered her life and the lives of her husband and children. Dr. Spohn brought Julie to Rocky River for an appointment with Dr. Nemeh, and in one session, Julie got her miracle. Suddenly Julie could once again walk, talk, and eat more normally, and her cognitive processes were unscrambled.

On Valentine's Day 2008, *Good Company* featured this amazing story of enduring love and physical transformation in a "one year later" special. Dr. and Mrs. Spohn were interviewed live in WKYC-TV 3's downtown Cleveland studios by program hostess Andrea Vecchio. *Good Company* aired photographs of Julie's heartbreaking condition prior to meeting Dr. Nemeh.

Until the Spohn story, Dr. Nemeh had consistently been uninterested in appearing live on television. He reconsidered when Channel 3 producer Terry Moir proposed an on-air surprise reunion of Dr. Nemeh with his patient and her husband. Issam liked the idea of honoring this couple whose faith in God and love for each other had sustained them through thirteen difficult years, so he agreed to make an unannounced visit to the set. When the day came, Terry kept the doctor secluded in a separate room until the Spohn story had been told. After a commercial break, Terry led him into the studio, and, while cameras rolled, Dr. Nemeh surprised Gregory, Julie, and Andrea by joining them on the set for an emotional celebration of God's healing touch.

Issam Nemeh's parents, Wadi and Nadia Nemeh, married sixty-two years, would agree there is something very special about their son. Born on April 10, 1954, in Homs, Syria, both parents remember Issam being an unusually calm baby. The name Issam means "one who has always a good stand; one who is solid in everything." Neither mother nor father can recall him crying or fussing; he lay in his crib amusing himself rather than howling for his mother. As a child he was exceptionally spiritual, often spending hours at St. Vincent's Church located about a mile from home, where he would pray or talk with the parish priest.

On the playground, Issam displayed a unique compassion as well as undoubting faith. If a child fell or was hurt, Issam would trot over to the child and just stand there. He never told anyone what he was doing. He just did it. He was praying for the hurt to go away.

He was still a youth when he first received a calling to bring people closer to God. Later, in his second year of high school, Issam says the message became clearer and he knew that a religious mission lay before him. The word "religion" comes from the Latin *religare,* or, "retying"; thus religion is the science of reconnecting souls to their Creator. At fifteen, then, Issam understood that his destiny was to bring people back into a living relationship with God. "That part," he says, "was pre-destined for me." He also knew then that a significant event would have something to do with Saul of Tarsus—the Jew who was converted to Christianity while traveling on the road to Damascus—who became the apostle Paul with whom he felt a great affinity.

In school Issam excelled in math, science, and languages. Following high school graduation, Issam attended a one-year premed course of study at the Zabrze campus of the Medical University of Silesia in Poland, after which he completed six years of study and attained his medical degree in 1980. He then traveled to Germany to do medical rotations. Issam returned to Damascus in the summer of 1982, a time of political and social upheaval, and told his father he had received a message from God telling him he must get to America. Wadi was astonished. He told Issam, "Son, you'll never get a visa! It's impossible! They're turning down all the Christians."

"I'll get one."

Issam went to the American consulate to apply for a visa. The consul general told him to come back the next day. When Issam relayed the day's events to his father, Wadi was unimpressed. "His words mean nothing. 'Come back tomorrow.' It will be the same story no matter how many tomorrows you go back."

The next day, Issam presented himself at the consulate. The consul general, who was just outside the embassy, spotted him, walked over to the young doctor, put his arm around his shoulder and escorted him into his office. He gave Issam the one and only visa he awarded that day.

Soon after receiving his visa, Issam boarded a plane to America, where he stayed a short while with Dr. Paul Boz, a friend of the Nemeh family, in California. Next, he flew to Ohio to visit his father's cousin, Dr. Michael Hanna, whose admiration for Wadi Nemeh was great. Issam decided to make Cleveland his home.

Between 1983 and 1985 Issam completed a general surgery residency at Fairview General Hospital, followed by a three-year residency in anesthesia at Huron Road Hospital. He practiced anesthesiology until, in 1992, he left the field to open an acupuncture practice. He saw in his new chosen specialty the opportunity to spend more time with his patients.

In the course of the acupuncture session Dr. Nemeh has time to develop a robust doctor-patient relationship in which he serves as counselor, teacher, and physician. As he sees it, his most important function is as a spiritual guide, and he fulfills one part of this role by using the session to pray for his patient. Thus, while Dr. Nemeh treats the physiology of his patients with a procedure designed to close the gates along the pathway of pain, he is at the same time treating their spiritual life with prayer designed to open the gates to the real healer: God.

Throughout his life, Issam maintained a steady focus on prayer even as he completed rigorous studies under challenging circumstances and relocated to a new country. During the steady dialogue of his prayers, Issam kept the ear of his soul closely attuned to God's messages. He made life-altering decisions that sometimes seemed irrational because he allowed himself to be led by God, step by step, ever more closely to the time and the place when his gift of faith would help reconnect thousands of people to their Creator.

II.

❧

Prayer

Time no longer means anything in such prayer, which is carried on in instants of its own, instants that can last a second or an hour without our being able to distinguish one from another . . . Pure prayer only takes possession of our hearts for good when we no longer desire any special light or grace or consolation for ourselves, and pray without any thought of our own satisfaction.

—Thomas Merton, *No Man Is an Island*

People struggle to find words that can adequately define who Dr. Nemeh is to them. His parents noticed an exceptionally well developed sense of serenity from the time of his birth, and they say that as he grew his spiritual sophistication seemed to increase exponentially. Others variously describe him as a saint, a prophet, a conduit of God's love, and a physician of unshakable faith. However, one word—"compassionate"—recurs over and over again in descriptions given by those who meet him, become his patients, or are prayed over by him. People say they see in his eyes, facial expressiveness, and body language something that tells them *Here is a supremely compassionate man.* In this society, it is unusual to receive unconditional love from anyone, and yet unconditional acceptance, love, and compassion are what Dr. Nemeh proffers to everyone.

That he is different is indisputable. The question that remains is, why? Why does Dr. Nemeh exude so distinctive an air of otherworldliness, and how are we to understand a compassion so expansive and unbounded as his? Why is it so hard to describe him?

Dr. Nemeh has spent many of his waking hours for most of his life engaged in prayer. He may be a medical doctor but he is also a "professional pray-er." Like advanced meditators and those who engage for long periods of time in contemplative practices, Dr. Nemeh has developed strong connections to the spiritual dimensions of life, and his experience of the real world is shaped by this facile relationship with spirituality.

Thomas Merton was a twentieth-century American Trappist monk and social activist whose prolific writings (more than seventy books, more than two thousand poems, and numerous essays and journals) have solidified his reputation as a great thinker as well as a devout man of God. Although his religious identity was Roman Catholic, he focused on promoting understanding of and tolerance among practitioners of different religions. Decades after his death in 1968, he continues to inspire spiritual seekers the world over.

Merton's quintessential accomplishment was to share a view into the transformative experience of mystical union with God. Prayer, for Merton, is the most worthy of all activities in which a human can engage, with rewards that are twofold: contact with God, and the attainment of the most elevated expression and highest actualization of one's own self.

Today, the subject of the innermost intricacies of prayer

has extended from monasteries to microscopes as pioneering researchers carve out a new field of study called "neurotheology" from the existing fields of biology, neurology, psychology, and theology. At the University of Pennsylvania, Andrew Newberg, M.D., directs the Center for Spirituality and the Mind, and he brings better than fifteen years of experience to this interdisciplinary field. Using diverse methods, Dr. Newberg and his colleagues offer compelling evidence of the interfacing of science and faith. Their studies of people who meditate or pray for long periods every day over the course of numerous years show changes in brain structures at the neuronal level. Furthermore, these researchers have found that the longer and more frequently one is engaged in meditation or prayer, the more extensive are the changes in the brain structures.

Specifically, brain-scan studies have shown that prayer has the effect of stimulating the anterior cingulate, the center of the nervous system in which the sensitive balance between thought and feeling is sustained. As prayer "exercises" the anterior cingulate—stimulating, strengthening, and enlarging it—there is a corresponding lessening of stimulation in the limbic system, where emotions like anger are processed. One way of viewing prayer, then, is that it strengthens and empowers the anterior cingulate, which thereby enables the empathy and compassion that are its specialties to override the more destructive, less rational reactions of the limbic system.

The contemplative practices of dedicated pray-ers like Thomas Merton and Issam Nemeh thus effect physiological alterations in their brain structures. There is a behavioral component to these changes. Scientists have correlated a highly stimulated anterior cingulate with a particular kind of personality. Simply stated, neurotheology studies suggest that the idea of God is a good influence on the wiring and functioning of our brains, because those who practice the art of praying are characterized by enhanced cognitive abilities, and, perhaps more important, by greater empathy and compassion as compared with people who do not meditate or pray.

Science, then, is catching up to great thinkers like Merton. When philosophers such as Merton offer written articulation of the ineffable encounters they have experienced, and the physiology of their perceived sensations are documented by these new brain-scan studies, the transformative nature of pure prayer becomes a little less mysterious. Prayer practices formerly illuminated by the quiet candle of solitary introspection can now be examined under the incandescent bulbs of the laboratory, with one shedding light upon what it *feels* like to experience God in the world, and the other revealing what it actually *looks* like physiologically when people engage in deep meditation or intense prayer.

Merton, as well as many meditation practitioners, described moments of transcendence during intense prayer as characterized by feelings of selflessness and timelessness. Again, brain-scan studies demonstrate at a structural level why this is so. During prayer, activity in the parietal lobe decreases, and one of the results of the decrease in activity in the parietal lobe is an augmented perception of timelessness and spacelessness.

Thus, the insights of neurotheology studies lend scientific credence to what holy men and prophets have said for millennia: prayer changes your life for the better, and there is a physiological basis that suggests why this is so. The brain becomes less adept at feeling anger, anxiety, aggression, and fear when it becomes more practiced at feeling empathy, compassion and love.

So, if Issam Nemeh seems to inhabit an introspective reality different from the norm, neurotheologists would theorize that an exceptionally exercised anterior cingulate would account for his consummate compassion, empathy, feelings of love and acceptance, and ability to interface with patients within the battleground of their suffering.

And make him very difficult to describe.

12.

Time in His Hands

Dr. Nemeh receives notes, cards, and letters of gratitude every day from patients and people who have come to healing services. One day during the summer of 2007 Maureen Leimkuehler, who volunteers as an usher at healing services, was visiting with Kathy at Dr. Nemeh's office. Kathy read aloud a letter in which a powerful healing was described, praise for God was offered, and gratitude was extended to Dr. Nemeh for his prayers on behalf of the letter writer. Maureen was touched. She asked Kathy how many letters such as this they had received, and Kathy told her that a number of clear plastic boxes filled with notes and letters were in storage. Maureen adopted as her pet project the compilation of this vast collection of thank-you letters into scrapbooks.

Certain motifs can be found in these letters, such as the surprise healing of something not on a patient's "wish list." For example, on April 22, 2007, Georgia Leventis traveled from her home in Michigan to a healing service at Sts. Peter and Paul in Garfield Heights, Ohio. Georgia's goddaughter, Katie Avouris, came along, bringing what she said was a long list of things to pray for. Fifteen minutes after her prayer from Dr. Nemeh,

Katie was astonished when complete neurological sensation had been restored to a hand in which she had experienced numbness for seven years. Wonderful though it was, she and Georgia quickly realized that there was a "big picture message" in this healing. Katie had become so accustomed to the lack of feeling in her hand that she had not even placed this complaint on the list of things for which she was praying. God had captured her attention in a unique and powerful way with this "surprise" healing.

Another theme noted by many people who have written letters to the Nemehs is the out-of-body sensations experienced by patients during appointments with the doctor. Patients say they are woefully inaccurate at judging the length of their treatment sessions.

Dr. Nemeh's practice operates in a way that is uncommon because he works, he says, on the Holy Spirit's timetable. "I know when the Spirit has finished because I feel the ebb and flow of the Spirit in my hands." The appointment secretary accommodates these fluctuations by staying in touch with all but the first patient of the day regarding the estimated time treatment will begin. This way, patients know when to gauge their departure from home. If, say, a patient makes an appointment for four in the afternoon but the doctor has spent twice as much time with his one o'clock patient, the office secretary will advise the incoming patient to arrive at five rather than four.

One would expect that the mix of profound illness and concomitant desperation Dr. Nemeh sees every day, together with unpredictable appointment times and long waits, might create a combustible situation in the waiting room. That doesn't happen. When the doctor is treating a patient, what matters is the here and now of what is happening. Dr. Nemeh's attitude is that compared to being cured, or the alleviation of pain, or a health crisis being solved, what are mere minutes? They are but grains of sand. He says that when he prays he goes to a place where time is irrelevant, so he is incapable of hurrying a treatment.

Jane Coury stepped in as a volunteer office assistant in 2005. She had come to the doctor with various medical concerns in 2002; during her first appointment she experienced life-altering physical, emotional, *and* spiritual healings. From that day forward she considered Dr. Nemeh "her" doctor. After the Ted Henry news features aired in 2004 and 2005, Jane knew from her experience as a patient that the doctor and Kathy would need extra help at the office. "They were inundated with calls," Jane recalls. "They were booking almost a year in advance at the time of the Ted Henry story. I was there from ten in the morning until two or three the next morning on the days when I came to help out.

"Sometimes I felt it if someone was getting a miracle over in the treatment room. I would feel a calm, soothing, heated presence two rooms away from the scheduling office. I would ask him when he came out, 'Doctor, was a miracle happening in there?' and he would say, 'Yes.' Then the patient would come out free of pain and looking transformed. I think Dr. Nemeh is blessed; I think he is a saint, sent here by God. He is a servant of God. And this," she says, referring to his office, "is a place of reverence. Holy ground."

Time. Issam looks at people with his faraway eyes and they become a little uncomfortable. It's because they are struck by the unnerving idea that time means something different for him.

Ron Russell, owner of a business that is ranked among the top one hundred largest independent real estate companies in the country, came to know Dr. Nemeh through his wife, Debbie. Debbie sought treatment from Dr. Nemeh for a debilitating degenerative disc disease so disabling she was in bed for ninety days. Debbie was able to tolerate the excruciating pain only with the help of OxyContin, a strong narcotic similar to morphine. Doctors at the Cleveland Clinic told her she had bilateral neuroforaminal compromise, or, loss of disc space height, at C3 to C4, C4 to C5, and C5 to C6.

With three visits to Dr. Nemeh, however, Debbie was out of bed and completely off painkillers. Impressed with the doctor and his mission, Ron became a steady volunteer. He has often pondered that faraway-and-long-ago look in Dr. Nemeh's eyes.

He asked the doctor, "How can you sit in this office from early in the morning until God only knows when, day after day? How can you do it?"

"Time is irrelevant," responded Dr. Nemeh.

Ron reflected on that and concluded, "He's right. When he is praying, time doesn't matter. People see time through tunnel vision. The doc operates outside that tunnel. When I am at a healing service I don't notice time. I am here but not just physically and mentally. There is another dimension.

"I have always been the quintessential appointment person who lives his life boom-boom-boom going from one appointment to another. I am very good at time management. But when I am catching at a healing service, I get out of the regular time dimension. I'll look at the clock and it's one. What seems like ten minutes later I look again and it's four. It's not often that this kind of thing happens in life."

Dr. Nemeh explains that when he is praying he operates in a zone in which the Holy Spirit is present, and he loses all perception of time. When he is at prayer and he is feeling the presence of the Holy Spirit, time feels non-linear, bendable, and irrelevant for both doctor and patient. His prayers seem to belong, as Merton would say, less to time than they do to eternity.

No wonder he has faraway eyes.

꧂

13

To Journey, To Surrender

D r. Nemeh confesses he does not present personal petitions to the Lord. "God knows anyway," he says. "I don't need to ask." Although he advises his patients, "Go to God and ask Him to heal you," Dr. Nemeh will not do so for his own benefit. "It's like we have this agreement: I say to Him, 'I'm expecting it from You but I'm not going to ask.' And He always hears me. What is important is the love of God. We must realize one thing over all: we must love God and surrender ourselves to Him. He looks at you and sees you are capable of shining. He *wants* to see you shining. The only one I cannot help is myself. Otherwise there are no limitations on my prayer because I have supreme trust. I know He won't let me down as long as He is using me."

This concept of being used seems antithetical to a contemporary mind-set, but Dr. Nemeh is comfortable with it. He says that long ago he gave up every earthly ambition in order to serve God. "I'm so devoted to Him, I am ready to surrender completely my physical life for Him. When we surrender, as St. John taught us, the Father will be in awe, and we will be like the Son to Him. It's not hard to attain—that's God's promise to us. Everything just depends on the approach we have toward God. Most people come to God and ask for blessings or healings they will use for their own purposes. Their humanness gets in the way. They are not focused on the way they should behave. They don't look to God from a perspective of being His servant."

There is a selflessness in Dr. Nemeh that he shows in part by the way he is able to "exit" the physical self, as he describes it, so that he can meet his patients' needs. He says, "I could not do this, day after day for all these hours, unless the Holy Spirit lifted me."

He also says he knows he may have only one chance with a patient and considers each session a precious opportunity. He has a well-developed awareness of an additional layer of responsibility within the doctor-patient relationship. He approaches his job with the physician's goal of bringing his patients to a state of physical and mental well-being, but there is more.

Although some people visit the doctor only once, others come back again and again, returning because they find themselves involved in a succession of healings throughout years of challenges, injury, and spiritual development. Typically, they come to realize that if the original cure they sought had been achieved instantaneously, they would have been cheated out of a much fuller healing experience.

Audie Kiplinger has been a patient of Dr. Nemeh's for over ten years. She was diagnosed with stage IV non-Hodgkin's lymphoma in 1994. After eight months of chemotherapy, she went into remission. On March 13, 1996, she slipped and fell, breaking her tibia and fibula. Pins and screws were surgically inserted into her ankle and the foot calcified abnormally, in such a way that it turned to the left, leaving her with an ungainly limp. Walking was an excruciating exertion and she could not maneuver stairs. She was so crippled, when she and her husband built a downsized, empty-nester home, they were forced to include an elevator in the floor plans so that Audie would be able to reach the different levels of their home. A specialist recommended that the foot be fused into a permanently left-turning position. Because one of Audie's great delights in life is golf, she refused to submit to a procedure that would have created a permanent physical handicap.

A friend told her about Dr. Nemeh. At Audie's first appointment with him on October 27, 1997, which lasted two hours, her left-turning foot straightened in a partial healing—the foot was not quite back to its original state, structurally speaking, but the process of full healing had been initiated.

"Two days after that Monday appointment," Audie says, "I walked up and down the stairs to the lower level of our home for the very first time!" What amazed her even more was the "bonus blessings" she experienced. "My scoliosis was corrected and my varicose veins were treated and improved," she says. "Plus, after this first appointment, I had no pain in my back! I was able to do some gardening for the first time in a long time—without any pain! It was a *miraculous* healing!"

Dr. Nemeh told her he wanted to work on decalcifying her injured foot, and Audie was all for it. She began acupuncture treatments three times a week that were reduced, with progress, to once a week. Then, over a period of a couple of years, Dr. Nemeh stepped her treatments down to twice a month and, finally, once a month. What kept her coming back? "The healings, both physical and spiritual; the friendship; and the experiences," says Audie. "All." Eventually, Audie's foot was restored to its pre-injury condition.

Audie came out of remission and spent four years in and out of various chemotherapies. "My office visits to Dr. Nemeh became so much a part of my life. He always gave me relief until the next appointment. Physically, he helped me to feel better. He helped me spiritually and emotionally even more.

"The way I look at my many years of coming to Dr. Nemeh is that if I had been completely healed at the first visit, I wouldn't have gotten to know him. But that was not in God's plan. My foot was just the entryway to the real reason I was meant to come.

"I should have been gone by now; every year is a gift. But I wouldn't change a thing about what I've been through because everything was a stepping-stone to now. I learned so much from Issam. I learned that when you concentrate on helping others, as he does, you lose your own agenda. I learned from him how not to think about myself."

Dr. Nemeh is aware that he is very involved in the healing process of his patients. "Every person is a completely separate case and every journey is so different. I go on the journey with them, . . . and sometimes it's not a happy one. Sometimes, I cry inside. I get so frustrated and I want them to *get there*." When patients do not receive a physical healing, family members shake their heads and ask, "Why not my loved one?" Dr. Nemeh says there is always a reason.

Case in point: Dr. Nemeh offered long-distance telephone prayers for an eighty-five-year-old woman living in Arizona. Crippled from congestive heart failure and asthma, Catherine was also besieged by a multitude of other frustrating health issues, including the deterioration of her vision, which robbed her of the ability to read, which was her chief daily pleasure.

Her faith was strong, and she had always believed in the power of prayer. In fact, she believed that her primary task at this stage of her life was to pray for others, especially her children and their families. When Dr. Nemeh prayed, he said he knew she had cultivated an active relationship with God because he felt "connected" to her. He was not surprised when Catherine told him she felt electricity coursing through her body during the prayer.

Catherine had been watching a closed-captioned documentary television program when she received the call from the doctor. As Dr. Nemeh prayed, Catherine exclaimed, "I can read the words! I can read the words on the television! I couldn't read them before—now I can!"

The next time Dr. Nemeh prayed a telephone prayer over Catherine, it seems a healing of the heart occurred—but it was not a healing of her diseased organ. For eight years she had carried unresolved bitterness in her heart, a destructive grudge against her daughter-in-law, a loyal and loving woman who did not deserve Catherine's anger. After this prayer session with Dr. Nemeh, Catherine picked up the phone, called her son's widow, and apologized.

"Sometimes intervention is necessary to save the soul," Issam says. "If someone harbors bitterness in his or her heart, the healing process necessarily becomes an interior one; it is more important that the bitterness is resolved and forgiveness enters the heart than that the person receive a physical healing."

Dr. Nemeh has seen some patients who want their healing

so they can continue living their lives along the same trajectory they had been following. "They do not see in their illness God's invitation to step up to a higher challenge. They don't appreciate the opportunity He is holding out to them. They do not see that He is asking them to surrender their life to His purpose." Dr. Nemeh believes a full healing eludes these people because they don't see the beauty in changing their approach to life and focusing more on serving God.

Dr. Nemeh believes healing depends on the person's state of mind. "The approach to God is the most important thing— and by approach I mean love for Him, trust in Him, and surrender to Him. I surrender totally to the will of God. I offer Him my life. I promise Him my life. I am His servant. That is my approach."

Indeed, Dr. Nemeh seems to have an uncanny ability to view discouraging events and challenges with calm detachment. He says the difficulties with which he is faced are opportunities to shine for God. Because of his highly developed empathic sensitivity he suffers along with his patients. He endures, he says, by offering the pain he feels as a sacrifice to God the Father in honor of His Son. "We must see God's will in everything that happens in our daily life. We need to see Him in *everything* small and large—*that's* the true love of God! When we reach that level it means that we honestly love and trust Him."

14.

᭟

The Missing Piece

D r. Nemeh accepts that people are cured of disease, sickness, pain, and disfigurement by standard medical model treatments. He knows this is true; after all, he is licensed in anesthesiology and general surgery. "To cure someone," he explains, "is to successfully treat and solve the medical problems facing patients by means of known medical procedures and medicines. When the cure eludes physicians, it means there is a missing element. When medication and medical treatment do not have the complete effect, you add prayer. Prayer is sometimes the missing piece that can complete a healing."

Working Monday through Saturday from nine in the morning until midnight leaves Dr. Nemeh little time to be out in the community. Kathy has been known to arrange an office luncheon so that people who wish to meet the doctor can do so. Father Joseph Fata of St. Luke Catholic Church in Boardman, Ohio, met with the Nemehs at one such lunch.

Father Fata had heard that his friend Father Brad Helman had hosted a healing service with Dr. Nemeh at St. Michael's in Canton. Father Helman told Father Fata that his parishioners had lobbied for the service and that the response was phenomenal. "We had no trouble getting more than a hundred volunteers," Father Helman said. "The impact of the healing day is far beyond my expectations. People are returning to church and they're all talking about it. They want to have Dr. Nemeh back again as soon as possible."

Father Fata said, "Okay, that settles it! I have to look into this." He telephoned Kathy and told her, "I'm looking for something that will inject some new spirit and involvement into the parish."

She invited him to come to lunch at the office to meet the doctor and some of the ministry volunteers. Father Fata stayed for four hours, talking with Dr. Nemeh in between patients. He mentioned in passing that he was dealing with a health issue but never said anything about cancer. Near the end of the afternoon Kathy asked if he would like the doctor to pray over him. He replied, "I had lunch; I had dessert; I may as well get whatever else is on the menu!"

Issam finished with a patient and once again rejoined the group gathered around the lunch table. Dr. Nemeh stood before the priest. He had no knowledge of the priest's recent battle with prostate cancer, yet when he started his prayer his hands went straight to the place where Father Fata had just had surgery. The priest vaguely experienced a sensation of falling. Two men standing nearby acted as catchers and lowered him into a chair. He lost awareness of everyone and everything in the room.

After he came to, Father Fata had a crying jag. He couldn't understand this bizarre reaction. "I'm not crying; I'm not feeling sadness or joy. There are just these tears!" He left the office having promised the Nemehs that he would think about hosting a healing service at St. Luke's Church. He did.

He thought a lot about the Nemehs. He decided he liked these people and returned for one more lunch. Issam again prayed over him. He experienced another emotional outpouring and, as before, did not understand what was happening or why. "I interpreted this as a sign," he said. "I decided this ministry could touch my parishioners in ways similar to how it was touching me."

Father Fata scheduled a healing service. He also decided he would like to include Dr. Nemeh in his own team of specialists.

Five years earlier Father Fata had been diagnosed with bladder cancer. He endured one year of decidedly unpleasant treatment and then the cancer showed up in the prostate gland. Surgery was advised.

"The goal is to give you twenty more years of life," his doctor told him.

"Sounds good to me."

He underwent eight hours of surgery.

"During that time I was held up in prayer by so many people," said the priest. "This is a phenomenal parish. I actually felt the prayer *physically*. My surgeon told me he prays before every surgery, and mine was quite successful. I recuperated and returned six months later for tests."

Every series of postsurgical tests came back positive for new cancer cells. His doctor suspected the cancer might be coming from the kidneys, but there was a problem in determining if his hunch was correct: Father Fata believed he could not tolerate the dye visualization diagnostic because he had a life-threatening allergy to the dye. He and his doctor were paralyzed between two unsatisfactory situations: not knowing if the cancer was in the kidneys; and fearing that if he were to undergo the test that would show what they needed to know about his kidneys, it could be lethal. At this point in his journey through the labyrinth that is cancer treatment, the priest met the Nemehs and scheduled some treatment time with the doctor.

Dr. Nemeh never suggested that Father Fata alter his medical regimen in any way. When Father Fata expressed his inclination to refuse the dye visualization test Dr. Nemeh advised him otherwise. "Do it," he urged. "Take the test. You will be okay." On the strength of Dr. Nemeh's confidence, Father Fata called the doctor's office and asked them to schedule the procedure. He survived the test.

For Father Fata, as for Dr. Nemeh, medicine and spirituality are not separate entities but different facets of one continuum. He says that Issam views what he is doing as a science. "Dr. Nemeh is a seer into the human organism. It's not just hocus-pocus to him. That resonates with me," he says. "Theology is a science: it's the science of faith. And there is medical science. If I had a successful procedure, why does it have to be one or the other? Why can't it be a combination of both?" Father Fata gives credit to both medicine and prayer for the happy outcome of this important procedure.

During his stressful confrontation with bladder and prostate cancer, Father Fata says he turned to prayer and his parishioners for support. "When you let God into the whole picture, you can be a little less concerned about the details. Now I'm changed. I'm more at peace. Details used to make me nuts, but I realize now that none of that stuff is important."

Father Fata scheduled the first healing service for his parish on February 18, 2007. Many parishioners told him, "We're not sure about this, but we trust you." Father Fata anointed people with holy oil all throughout the day, and his parishioners interpreted this action as a sign that they could open their hearts and trust this new experience. Sonny Cascarelli, a devoted, active parishioner, had been blunt when Father Fata approached him to serve as a catcher. "Father," he told his pastor, "I don't believe in that crap." Nevertheless, Sonny wanted to support his priest, so he agreed to help out. He then spent the next few weeks grumbling about the notion of a healing service. Once he was in the middle of the service Sonny was so captivated by the intense spirituality he was feeling, he stayed until the last person had been prayed over. Years later Sonny reminisced, "What I got out of it is everlasting. I have a whole different view of the Holy Spirit; the Spirit is part of my life. There's a different look to my religion now."

The type of spiritual growth Sonny verbalized was a refrain Father Fata would hear over and over again following the Nemeh healing service. "The impact was unimaginable," says Father Fata. "Not a week goes by that my parishioners don't ask me when the Nemehs will return. Even if there was no physical healing, people found they could better cope with their illness. They also became more willing to share their faith. They opened up in meetings and were willing to talk in ways they had never done before. Some were motivated to do a book study. The liturgy committee got a shot in the arm."

Clerical colleagues inquired about the event at their quarterly meeting and proposed an ecumenical celebration. Father Fata saw in their hunger possibilities for outreach to other religions. He decided to organize an ecumenical healing service. "Jesus came to show us the Father," says Father Fata. "To be *the Way*, not *the End*. That implies *movement*." He called the Nemehs and arranged to hold a service at St. Luke's Church on September 9, 2007, with equal participation by members of three other denominations. It was a watershed day.

Afterward Father Fata reflected on the impact the Nemeh healing service had on Boardman's faith community. "Dr. Nemeh reorders perspectives. Basically, everything he does points to a greater reality, and he always points everything to God, never to himself. He is saying, in effect, 'This isn't about me. This isn't even about the miracles.' And we get that. We get that this is about Jesus, who came to show us the Father—who came so that we could become closer to the Father."

Father Joseph Fata has given the Nemeh phenomenon a great deal of thought in the wake of his cancer and the St. Luke's healing services. "I see Issam Nemeh as a prophet. A prophet is someone who helps interpret the present. Dr. Nemeh has focused his life on being a prophet. He takes a sickness or a weakness, or an instability, or a joy, or a sorrow, and he shines a light on it so that you can understand it in your life. Sometimes that understanding brings about healings that we cannot anticipate. He fulfills this role of a prophet.

"A priest ministers one-on-one and to the whole community. That's what I do. A person of faith ministers *to that faith*. Dr. Nemeh is a person of faith."

Father Fata sees enormous potential in the Nemeh prayer ministry. "He must keep broadening the circle. Jesus did it with eleven men in a little corner of the world. He never traveled more than ten miles. I would say to Dr. Nemeh: 'Keep doing what you are doing—it is exactly what Jesus did. He touched individuals, one at a time.'"

Father Fata scheduled a third healing service for his parish in November 2008. This one was in celebration of the news that he was cancer-free.

15.

༈

Beginnings

It began with a phone call.

Sometime in 1999 Monica Marie Navin, a Sister of the Incarnate Word and Blessed Sacrament living in Parma Heights, Ohio, telephoned Dr. Nemeh's offices at Southwest General Health Center in Middleburg Heights, where he worked as an independent contractor in the Complementary Care Program. She asked if she could meet Dr. Nemeh. She had heard that he was a man of great faith, and was intrigued by the extraordinary testimonies from people who attended the convent's chapel. Kathy and Sister Monica arranged a meeting, and when Kathy and Issam arrived at the convent, the three talked for two hours of faith, miracles, healings, and the word of God. Sister Monica declared she was so inspired she invited the couple to the next weekly Wednesday evening service held at her convent chapel.

They came.

At the Mass, Sister introduced the doctor by saying, "This is Dr. Nemeh, who is here with his wife. I would like to invite him to pray with us tonight." Sister Monica and Dr. Nemeh prayed side by side over those who were in attendance. Sister Monica carried a large wooden crucifix, which she pressed firmly upon the person's shoulder as she began her prayer. Issam simply extended his hands, sometimes touching the person gently, and prayed.

After that night, Sister kept in close contact with Kathy and the doctor. When Southwest General Health Center closed the Complementary Care Program in late 1999, Dr. Nemeh opened a private practice on West 117th Street in Cleveland. Sister Monica would sometimes drop in for a quick, chatty visit if she was in the area. Kathy grew to love this spunky nun.

One day Kathy glanced out the office window and spotted Sister Monica's car. A few minutes later the nun breezed in, greeting Kathy by her Sister Monica–given nickname. "Katie Kelly," she called out.

"Sis," Kathy replied.

"Katie Kelly, I don't know how to explain this but I got a message from God telling me that I should come and see 'Himself' and that he would know what I need."

At that moment the doctor popped out of the treatment room to fetch something for the patient he was treating, spied Sister Monica, and instructed Kathy to tell Sister to stay for a treatment.

This commotion was very amazing to the woman sitting in the waiting room who held the next appointment. This patient had come to Dr. Nemeh because she was suffering terrible pain in her right knee. Yet she spontaneously gave up her appointment hour to Sister Monica. Surprised at her own outburst, the woman covered her mouth with her hand. This was no small offering; there is no predicting the length of time Dr. Nemeh might spend with any patient.

"There you are, in terrible pain, and you give your time to Sister," Kathy commented to the woman. "God bless you!"

While Sister was in the treatment room the woman's injured knee began radiating with heat. The heat pulsated until the throbbing in her knee subsided and she was pain-free. Incredulous, she told Kathy what had just happened. "The Holy Spirit can do anything," Kathy explained with a smile. "You got a healing because your heart was pure. You were generous to Sister and God noticed." The woman and Kathy agreed she no longer needed a treatment from the doctor, and she went home.

In the meantime Dr. Nemeh had made an alarming discovery. He came out of the treatment room and told Kathy, "Sister needs an ear, nose, and throat specialist right away. I have found a mass at her neckline; there is no time to lose."

Sister broke in. "I really don't trust any other doctor like I trust you, but I have an ear, nose, and throat doctor in Parma."

Dr. Nemeh shook his head. "No, you need the absolute best. Not just any doctor will do." Sister argued that she should use her doctor because of her insurance coverage, and she prevailed. They secured an appointment for her for the next day. When Sister left, Dr. Nemeh told Kathy, "It's very bad. Sister has cancer, one of the worst kinds."

Sister's ear, nose, and throat doctor in Parma held up his hands and said, "This is way beyond me. You need the best specialist in Cleveland. Call me back and let me know how things go."

"Yes, Doctor. Amen and God bless you," Sister said.

Sister Monica then consulted with doctor number three.

He ordered an MRI and a CAT scan. One of the nurses working at his office offered encouragement. "Sister, do you see that sign on the wall? It says, 'We treat; Jesus heals.'"

"Well then, I would say I'm in the right place," Sister Monica replied.

Tests revealed exactly what Dr. Nemeh suspected: adenocarcinoma of the parotid gland. It was a huge cancerous tumor and it was intricately entwined with her facial nerve. The surgeon explained that the operation would be difficult. He would have no choice but to sever the facial nerve, forever giving her the appearance of a stroke victim. She would have to learn to talk again and would undergo cancer treatment five days a week for five weeks.

Kathy was devastated when the test results arrived by fax. Crying, she brought the records to Issam, but he reassured her, "There is no need for tears. God is going to heal her. I know it."

The day of her surgery, at two in the morning, Dr. Nemeh gave Sister Monica one last preoperative treatment. As he was administering acupuncture and praying, Sister Monica confided, "Well, I'm ready for this and for whatever God sends me." No sooner than those words were out, she felt something pop inside her neck and the skin on her neck became bright red.

When they said good-bye, Sister Monica's parting words to Dr. Nemeh were, "I know Jesus heals."

Thursday morning, when the surgeon opened her up, he found Sister Monica's tumor was no longer encased in a mass of entwined nerves. He was able to remove the cancerous mass without disturbing the delicate nerves that control the facial muscles.

Mother Superior was with Sister Monica in the recovery

room when a nurse appeared carrying a tray of food. Incredulous, Mother Superior exclaimed, "That can't be for Sister!" It was. Sister Monica called the Nemehs from the recovery room, chortling when Kathy answered the phone.

"Katie Kelly."

"Sis."

"I'm sitting up and I'm eating Jell-O."

"What?"

"The doctor can't believe it. He took out the tumor and he told me the facial nerve was back where it should be. I'm going home tomorrow."

Kathy put Dr. Nemeh on the phone with Sister. He was jubilant and praised God for the wonderful news. Sister told him, "Thank you for sharing with me the healing powers that Jesus gave you." He recommended she come in just as soon as she was able. "I want to get rid of that scar for you," he told her.

The next day Sister Denise and Sister Elizabeth came to the hospital to bring her home. She actually tried to walk to the elevator. "Oh, my goodness, Sister Monica, please get into this wheelchair," they scolded. Twenty stitches ran up the side of her neck, the wound a gruesome display of the previous day's surgical work. But Sister Monica was unfazed. As she passed the nursing station, she called out, "Thank you, everyone! You have been very good to me!"

Two weeks later the surgeon gave her a stunning pathology report. "Sister, I don't know how to tell you this, but it's not cancer anymore. You've had . . . you've had a miracle." Sister Monica left his office with neither chemotherapy nor radiation in her future.

———

Jesuit Father Robert Welsh, president of Cleveland's St. Ignatius High School from 1979 to 2000, knew Sister Monica because his cousin also belonged to the Sisters of the Incarnate Word and Blessed Sacrament order. One day when he ran into Sister Monica she told him of her miracle. They put their heads together. "Why don't we have a Mass of Thanksgiving for my healing?" Sister suggested. "We can have Dr. Nemeh come, too." The two brought their proposal to "Katie Kelly" and she loved the idea.

Sister Monica called her friends Brother Dale and Brother David, members of the Brothers of the Holy Spirit, who have a chapel outfitted with a tabernacle, altar, and seventy-five chairs in the basement of their Brooklyn, Ohio, residence. Father Welsh and Sister Monica extended word-of-mouth invitations and in November 1999 there was standing room only for Father Welsh's Thanksgiving Mass. After the Mass a chair was placed in front of the altar and those wishing to receive a prayer took turns sitting in it while Dr. Nemeh and Sister Monica prayed over them. That simple service was the nearly unnoticed beginning of Dr. Nemeh's public prayer ministry.

The new ministry might have stopped there but Sister Monica, Father Welsh, and Kathy were inundated. Acquaintances heard about what had happened from the people who had been at the Thanksgiving service and they complained, "Why didn't you call me?" Others scolded, "I would have come in a heartbeat!" and "Next time let me know!" Sister Monica and Father Welsh organized a second Mass in the basement chapel. Again, there was standing room only. Again, a clamor arose from those who wished they had been invited. Clearly, there were many more people needing prayer.

A third Mass and healing prayer service was held in the

chapel of the Poor Clare Colettine Nuns' monastery. Kathy's father, Tony Ghazoul, and others lifted wheelchairs up the steps of the chapel. One hundred twenty-eight people jammed a room with a capacity of eighty-two.

Father Welsh watched the demand for prayers with a discerning eye. "Kathy," he said, "come to St. Ignatius and take a look at our St. Mary of the Assumption Chapel. Call me when you arrive on campus."

The contemporary chapel-in-the-round had been financed by visionary philanthropist Murlan J. "Jerry" Murphy, Sr., St. Ignatius Class of 1936. Jerry Murphy was the retired chairman of JTM Products, a family-owned industrial lubricant business most famous for manufacturing Murphy Oil Soap. Jerry had paid for the construction of two buildings important to the St. Ignatius community: the Murphy Field House, an intramural sports facility completed in 1993; and St. Mary of the Assumption Chapel, built in 1999. Chiseled in the chapel cornerstone is a Latin phrase, which, translated, means "That which soap has made."

One day during the construction phase of the chapel, Jerry was studying the blueprints along with his architects when his grandson Jimmy tugged on his sleeve. The men paused and listened to what Jimmy wanted to contribute. He told his grandfather they should cut a hole in the top of the ceiling so that Blessed Mother and angels would be able to get inside, and so that the prayers of the people could have a direct route out of the chapel, straight up to Heaven. The architects drew the child's idea into their plans.

The chapel is stunning. A floor-to-ceiling stained-glass mural dominates one entire wall. It is done in sumptuous shades of lavender and depicts the risen Christ greeting his overjoyed mother. Though there is beauty at every turn of the head, the ceiling, with its chevron-beam construction and circular skylight in the center, is the chapel's most memorable feature.

Kathy drove to the high school her two brothers, Myron and Johnny, had attended. Standing inside the chapel, she felt holiness pulsating. Eyes shining, she told Father Welsh, "It's perfect."

"When do you want it?"

"Mother's Day?"

"Great idea."

Kathy took her lifelong devotion to Blessed Mother and funneled it into a beautiful ceremony in Our Lady's honor. Father Welsh was the Mass celebrant. Sister Monica stepped to the microphone after the liturgy and told the story of her miracle. "You cannot do too much without prayer," she concluded. "Cardinal Cook said, 'Prayer is the greatest gift you can give someone.' So help others by giving them your prayers. And as far as Dr. Nemeh goes, he is a very prayerful person. He has great faith. God works within him in a very special way."

Throughout the afternoon, Dr. Nemeh prayed over approximately five hundred people, one by one.

The event on Mother's Day 2001 was so powerful that Father Welsh declared there was no choice but to do it again. In June of that year they held a Father's Day Mass and were gratified by the same standing-room-only response. Once a month thereafter, until the end of the year, Father Welsh offered Mass after which Dr. Nemeh prayed over people. Because so many were blessed with healings, the word spread, and approximately five hundred people hoping to be graced with a miracle of their own flocked to St. Mary of the Assumption Chapel for each subsequent event. Dr. Nemeh was not surprised by the high attendance at each service. He explains, "When people are in the same holy place, on board with similar prayers, it helps everyone's faith."

The prayer ministry grew in this way, quietly and out of the glare of publicity, like winter seeds sprouting under indoor grow lights. At seven different services held on the grounds of St. Ignatius High School in 2001, Dr. Nemeh prayed over approximately four thousand people. The following year, nine services were held at St. Mary of the Assumption Chapel and more than five thousand people received a prayer. Beneath the gorgeous chevron architecture of the skylight ceiling, this "accidental" prayer ministry began to establish its identity.

So many physical, emotional, and spiritual healings were being experienced by those who made a pilgrimage to St. Mary of the Assumption Chapel, parishioners from other churches began urging their pastors to invite Dr. Nemeh to their home parishes. The Nemehs went where God was calling them. During the next few years, Issam and Kathy were hosted by sixteen other Catholic and Christian churches. By March 2005, four years after Father Welsh celebrated that first Mass of Thanksgiving for Sister Monica's miracle, Dr. Nemeh had publicly prayed over nearly thirty thousand people. Then came the service on March 13, 2005, the day when more than ten thousand people packed Sts. Peter and Paul, after which two huge rain-check healing services were conducted at St. Bernadette's Church in Westlake.

16.

Rain Checks for Prayers

The first rain-check healing service was held on March 14, 2005, a mere thirteen hours after the conclusion of the service at Sts. Peter and Paul. Based on the numbered cards collected by volunteers working at the welcome tables in the lobby of St. Bernadette's, four thousand people received a prayer that day. Individual prayers continued from four in the afternoon on Monday until 5:50 Tuesday morning, only ten minutes shy of fourteen hours.

Zach Dever and his mother, Anne Dever, had come from Sandusky, Ohio, to Sts. Peter and Paul the day before but had left without having received their prayers. Anne drove her son nearly fifty miles to Westlake again the following day, she was so determined to bring Zach to Dr. Nemeh. No other doctor had been able to help her son.

Since the age of seven Zach had suffered from migraines so destructive they disrupted the normal course of his childhood. He was absent from school sometimes weeks at a stretch, which prevented him from establishing normal friendships. His headaches affected the entire family because they had to walk on tiptoe and hush their voices when Zach was in his bedroom nursing a headache.

After many years, his doctors at the Cleveland Clinic eventually recommended that he consult neurologists at the Michigan Head Pain and Neurological Institute. There, Zach experienced familiar frustrations. His parents and he would get excited when doctors prescribed a new drug or therapy, hopeful it would be the solution to his long struggle with head pain. Each new prescription was only a tease. An initial period of relief was quickly followed by complete dissipation of the drug's effectiveness. At the age of nineteen, Zach had lived half a life.

As Anne drove her son to St. Bernadette's for the rain-check healing service, Zach was in the painful throes of a marathon migraine. This one had lasted for four weeks.

Dr. Nemeh stepped to the tall young man in the prayer line and touched his head and neck. The doctor prayed a few words too soft for Zach to understand, and then Zach felt a warm rush throughout his entire body. He saw a white image of Jesus flash before his eyes. He was unaware that he drifted backward into the arms of a catcher who lowered him to the floor mat, where he lay oblivious to everything around him. When he came to, he and his mother returned to the pew and just sat for a while.

Finally, Zach said, "Wow. That was incredible." He struggled to find better words to describe it but could not. "Just incredible."

His mother asked him if his head hurt.

A smile lit his face when he realized the monthlong migraine was gone. "It's gone, Mom. I feel great." Mother and son drove home feeling a sense of awe.

Anne took Zach back to the Michigan Head Pain Institute

for what would be their last visit with the doctors who had tried so hard to help her son. When the doctors heard about the prayer that had ended Zach's headaches, they had nothing much to say except that they were glad Zach was free of pain.

The Dever family watched Dr. Nemeh's Web site for future healing services, and through the years they have become familiar faces in the prayer line. Kathy greets them with a big grin, sidles up to Zach, and asks, "How are you doing, Zach?" Each time, he has been able to say he remains migraine-free.

Headaches cannot be seen; they can only be felt. However, some manifestations that occurred at St. Bernadette's were plainly visible. Another mother, Joan Andrews, sought a healing miracle for her four-year-old son, Sean, who was born with a tumor just beneath his right eye. Doctors at a local hospital in Cleveland had advised that removing the unsightly tumor could cause more damage than leaving it there. They refused to operate unless the tumor changed in such a way that it threatened to cause blindness. Joan hoped for a better alternative for her son.

Dr. Nemeh pointed his finger at Sean's tumor and prayed, after which Joan and Sean returned to the pew. Within five minutes Joan glanced over at her son and could not contain her joy. Ushers, volunteers, and everyone sitting nearby heard her exclaim, over and over again, "Oh, my God! Oh, my God! It's gone! It's gone! It's *gone!!*" The tumor had vanished without a trace.

꒦

17

The Promise Is Kept

The next installment of the rain-check healing prayers was scheduled for five days later, on Saturday, March 19, which was the day before Palm Sunday. More than three thousand people turned in the hand-numbered cards they had held on to from the day spent at Sts. Peter and Paul. Again, as with the first rain-check healing service, each person received the prayer for which he or she had come.

Tricia Kaman was there. She was the portrait artist who had been so captivated by her first sight of the doctor and Kathy as they waded through the parting sea of people at the activity center. She arrived at St. Bernadette's very early to get a seat for the five o'clock Mass. She received her prayer at 5:30 the next morning. She stayed in that church more than fourteen hours for a prayer from Dr. Nemeh because she was desperate.

In September 2004 Tricia had been diagnosed with cervical spondylotic myelopathy (CSM), a degenerative disc disease that leads to narrowing of the spinal canal, which in turn results in chronic compression of the spinal cord, impaired blood flow, and neurological damage. The symptoms Tricia suffered were weakness, numbness, and lack of coordination in her arms, hands, and fingers; reduced fine motor control, especially in her fingers; radicular arm pain, or, referred pain from the spinal nerve roots; and changes in her gait. Her doctors advised her to undergo traction treatments on the DRX 9000 table for nonsurgical spinal decompression, which she halted after five and a half weeks when her neck pain became much more pronounced. In February 2005 she consulted another specialist, who prescribed a series of cortisone shots into the spine. At this point Tricia was in terrible pain every day. Her range of motion was nearly zero in her right arm. She couldn't dry her hair, it hurt to brush her teeth, and carrying a purse was excruciating. Yet she hesitated to get the shots. This therapy seemed so invasive. At a loss, her doctors could only suggest that she stop painting for two years, then come back for reevaluation.

Even greater than the pain was her fear of losing her identity as a portrait artist. *If I cannot paint, then who am I?*

Born in Sandusky, Ohio, Tricia grew up in the shadow of Cedar Point, a local megapark—an amusement park on steroids—a kind of midwestern Disney World. One ever-popular attraction is the portrait and caricature sketch huts sprinkled throughout the park. From the time Tricia was a little girl, her mother would pause in front of working artists and say, "Someday my daughter will draw here, just like you are doing." She was right.

When Tricia was fifteen, artist and concessionaire Ruth Price invited her to interview for a seasonal position at Cedar Point. Tricia brought a friend, Rich Kaman, to the interview. Mrs. Price put some materials in front of Tricia, then pointed to Rich and told Tricia, "Draw him." The portrait Tricia drew must have been adequate because she was hired on the spot. Cedar Point portraiture was Tricia's summer job until, on November 28, 1970, she married the same boy she had drawn for that interview. She assumed that her amusement park employment days were behind her.

But Mrs. Price called her out of the blue, asking her to come to Geauga Lake Park to participate in a meeting with the president, Gasper Lococo. At this meeting Mr. Lococo proposed that Tricia start up the first sketching enterprise at Geauga Lake. He was giving her the chance to develop her teenage internship at Cedar Point into a business of her own.

With this opportunity, Tricia founded Kaman's Art Shoppes. For a while she was a one-man band, drawing portraits at the park seven days a week. Mr. Lococo, who was known among his employees for strolling the grounds and checking to see that all was well, noticed. He took her aside and told her she had to hire other artists because he was worried she was testing her stamina. Tricia was touched by his concern. She placed ads in local newspapers and called classmates with whom she had attended art classes, and she hired other artists who would share the sketching shifts.

Thirty-nine years later, Tricia and Rich had raised two children and the company had grown substantially from its humble beginnings into a national organization with twenty-five hundred employees, a staff of seventy-five full-time managers, a graphics department, and in-house carpenters and wood burners who build the wooden structures that house the artistic supplies and provide an awning under which the artists sit while they draw. Tricia travels all over the country during the busy summer season when the parks are in full swing, visiting managers and giving on-the-spot drawing instruction to her artists.

Besides the amusement park business, Tricia also paints commissioned portraits in her studio in Murray Hill, a neighborhood renowned for both its superb restaurants featuring old-world Italian cuisine as well as its funky, bohemian vibe that attracts some of Cleveland's most talented artists. Clearly, painting is Tricia's life.

When doctors told her to lay down her brushes for two years, Tricia was devastated. Not paint? Impossible. Since Kaman's Art Shoppes is her livelihood, it was essential that she be able to travel, pull her suitcases through the airports, and tutor artists all over the country. Alleviating pain was only one portion of what motivated Tricia to seek a prayer from Dr. Nemeh. There was also the hope that her career, her joy, and her identity would be rescued from the ailment that threatened to tear apart the life she had constructed. There was no question that she would wait as long as fourteen hours for her prayer.

As dawn broke over St. Bernadette's Church, Tricia was signaled by a member of the Nemeh team to step up and take her place for a prayer. Kathy was praying just ahead of Issam, so she reached Tricia first. Kathy touched her lightly, said a word or two, and Tricia floated backward into the arms of her catcher. When Tricia's eyes opened and she once again became aware of her surroundings, she was helped to her feet and returned to her pew, where she sat feeling strange but somehow better.

After a few minutes, however, Tricia was flooded with feelings of distress. She turned to her pew mates, with whom she had become friendly during their nighttime vigil, and protested, "I have to get back up there! Dr. Nemeh never prayed over me!" Their answer surprised her. "Yes, he did," they said. "Dr. Nemeh put his hands on your stomach while you were lying on the floor!"

She was incredulous. *"Really?* He *prayed* over me?" She had not felt his hands.

"Yes, yes," they reiterated. "He prayed over you, Tricia!"

Tricia called Dr. Nemeh's office the following day. Her faith that he could help her was strong. She booked an appointment for the first available opening, which was more than four months away, the last week of July. Tricia felt a soaring sense of hope that after all she had suffered, Dr. Nemeh would be able to help. In July 2005, her hunch would be proven correct.

Patrick Coleman had missed the first St. Bernadette's healing service on Monday because he was on duty at the firehouse, but he rejoined the Nemeh team on the day before Palm Sunday to assist with crowd control, as he had on the Day of the Ten Thousand. In the wee hours of Sunday morning, there came a time when things were running smoothly out in the parking lot, so Patrick took the opportunity to step inside the church. It wasn't long before he was helping out as a catcher.

"Being that close to Issam," he says, "able to see the expressions washing over his face as he prayed, and feeling the heat radiating from the people as they fell into my arms—what an incredible experience!"

Catching allowed Patrick to view, up close, a side of the Nemehs that was new to him. He had never seen anything like Dr. Nemeh's intense concentration and the prayerful aura in which Dr. Nemeh moved. It seemed to him that there was a great deal of active suffering going on within the doctor's eyes.

Patrick quickly discovered that Kathy was very different from her husband. She conveyed compassion, that was true, and she was serious about her prayers over people, but at the same time she exuded irrepressible optimism. Patrick noticed that as Kathy came down the prayer line, the people over whom she prayed would fall into the arms of their catchers so fast it was sometimes hard to keep up with her.

Issam and Kathy prayed from five in the afternoon on Saturday, March 19, through the night until 8:50 a.m. on March 20, Palm Sunday morning. Neither remembers eating or taking a break.

The best estimates were that Dr. Nemeh had prayed over somewhere between three thousand and four thousand on March 13 at Sts. Peter and Paul; makeshift tickets helped track four thousand the following day at St. Bernadette's; and more than three thousand came to the second rain-check healing service. Between the three services, then, Dr. Nemeh had given individual prayers to more than ten thousand people.

When the second rain-check service was over and the last person had received his prayer, it never occurred to Issam that there were approximately the same number of people prayed over in the two rain-check healing services as had gone home from Sts. Peter and Paul without a prayer. In a week in which he had slept fewer than twenty hours, he had, in essence, done his best to redeem the promise made on March 13 that everyone would be prayed over.

Up on the altar that Sunday morning at St. Bernadette's, Father Weber began the liturgical celebration of Palm Sunday. The priest blessed palm fronds in commemoration of the day when Jesus was carried into Jerusalem on the back of a gray donkey colt, and the townspeople honored Him by laying palms and cloaks along the road the animal trod.

As he and Kathy left the church for home, a montage of faces and stupendous moments whirled like a kaleidoscope inside Issam's mind, and he wondered where and to whom God would next ask him to carry his faith.

⌇

18

The Gift of Peace

One feature of the Nemeh public prayer ministry is the absence of a systematic plan to follow up with the people over whom Dr. Nemeh has prayed. There is a mailing address and a Web site for those who wish to write to the Nemehs, but other than that, there is no outreach. Dr. Nemeh and Kathy merely show up at a church and pray.

When Dr. Nemeh is asked how many people were healed during that amazing week in March of 2005, his eyes widen, and he answers, "Four years later, we are still hearing stories about how God blessed people with healings!"

For example, it was not until the summer of 2009 that the Nemehs learned the details surrounding the death of a breast cancer patient, Jill Borowy Gadke. Jill had come to Sts. Peter and Paul on March 13, 2005, and received her prayer from Dr. Nemeh and Kathy while surrounded by twenty-nine of her family and friends. Through a complicated route of mutual acquaintances, Jill's cousin Michelle Walsh was introduced to Dr. and Kathy Nemeh in July 2009, and Michelle was able to fill them in on what happened during her cousin's final hours.

The story she told confirmed the healing power of prayer, even in the face of death.

Michelle recalled that Jill was glowing as they left Sts. Peter and Paul Church and was much better able to handle the physical suffering she would confront in the weeks ahead.

Michelle told the Nemehs about her last visit with Jill on April 24, 2005. She and her mother drove out to Jill's home, where Michelle's Aunt Kathy and Uncle Don were taking care of Jill while her husband was at work. When Michelle walked into Jill's room, clutching the present she had brought—a stuffed Goofy, Jill's favorite Disney character—Michelle was shocked. Jill was frail in a way no human being should ever be.

Jill grinned at the Goofy. Michelle put her arms around Jill and gave her a gentle hug.

"Don't be afraid," soothed Michelle. "We just have to believe that God is with you. God is carrying you and He will never let go of you."

In response, Jill pressed her arms around Michelle and gave her as strong a hug as she was able, her sign that she knew Michelle was talking about her impending death.

Michelle continued, "I'm praying for you, Jill. I love you and would do anything for you."

When it came time to say good-bye, Michelle gave her cousin a kiss and said, curiously, since Jill was clearly near the end of her journey, "I'll see you soon."

She then left the house feeling an irrational sense of urgency that something more must be done. She called her friend Randy Zinn, who she knew was active in the Nemeh ministry. Within the hour he gave her good news: bring Jill to Dr.

Nemeh's Rocky River office as soon as you can. Dr. Nemeh will see her right away.

Michelle started calling friends and family. By the time her uncle Don and aunt Kathy arrived at the doctor's office with Jill, twenty family members and friends were there to welcome them. Medication had bloated Jill almost beyond recognition, but even so as Jill's father lifted Jill from the car and into her wheelchair, Michelle saw hope burning brightly in her eyes.

Dr. Nemeh says, "Always, a prayer is heard." Yet it is also true that not always a prayer is answered in the way we would wish it to be.

Michelle's uncle and aunt stayed with their daughter during her acupuncture-plus-prayer treatment, but Michelle and company exited the tiny waiting room and spilled out into the corridor. Once again, just as when the group had settled in their pews surrounding Jill at Sts. Peter and Paul, and with no prompting, out came the rosaries. Twenty people plopped down on the floor in the hallway and quietly fingered their beads, praying that Jill's miracle was in the making. Inside the treatment room, however, Jill's father noticed Dr. Nemeh close his eyes and shake his head ever so slightly. That motion told him Jill was very near the end of her suffering.

Although Michelle felt as if the treatment lasted a lifetime, it was over in an hour. Jill's support group had pooled their resources to pay for the appointment, but when Michelle tried to settle up, the money was refused. The doctor had instructed his secretary not to accept any payment.

The family followed the wheelchair down the corridor to the elevator, and then out into the parking lot in a somber procession. Uncle Don lifted Jill into the car. Just before he closed the door on her, Michelle called out, "No—wait a minute! I didn't get to say good-bye!"

She reached in, hugged her cousin one last time, and said, "I love you."

"I love you, too," Jill replied.

The hope that had flared in Jill's eyes on the way in to her treatment had been rewarded. On the ride home Jill told her parents she had received the miracle of complete and total peace. The hour she had spent with Dr. Nemeh had infused her with a sense of serenity. She attributed this feeling of inner peace to a newly gained complete confidence in God and His plan. Jill accepted that, at the age of thirty-eight, the end of her life was near. Yet she was lifted to a higher spirituality that manifested in radiance.

Jill died that night.

Her parents were comforted that Jill died in this state of peace. The spiritual acceptance Jill felt in the last hours of her life was a huge gift to them because they had already buried one child. Their son, Bryan, was thirty-eight years old when he perished in a house fire on Thanksgiving Day 2000. Jill's parents had never stopped agonizing about what Bryan's final moments must have been like. In the years that followed Jill's death her parents grieved for their daughter each and every day, but because of the miracle of peace she experienced that last day, they were spared the unspeakable torment they had suffered over Bryan's brutal death.

When Michelle Walsh met Kathy and Dr. Nemeh four years after Jill passed away, she told them how much Dr. Nemeh's prayers had helped Jill, her family, and even Michelle because she had seen the great relief on her cousin's face after her appointment. She told them of the difference she heard in Jill's voice when Jill said good-bye.

"There are many miracles in Dr. Nemeh's healing services," Michelle says. "Sometimes these miracles are not an extension of health, wellness, and life here on earth. Sometimes it is a miracle in that the person he prays over comes to the true realization that God is leading her on a different journey. I know that Jill felt blessed by everyone who prayed for her and everyone who surrounded her; but the miracle everyone was hoping for turned into a blessing of a different kind. It was a miracle for Jill to feel God's peace and presence. It helped her accept that God was calling her home. Jill received not a miraculous transformation of health but a transformation of heart . . . and Dr. Nemeh's prayers brought her to that miracle of acceptance and understanding."

19

Sam's Gift

The next public healing service following the two rain-check services was supposed to take place at St. Mary of the Assumption Chapel. However, the four-hundred-seat capacity of the chapel was clearly not going to be sufficient for the numbers of people calling Dr. Nemeh's office asking for tickets. In fact, few facilities would be large enough.

Kathy began placing phone calls to find a larger venue for the April 3 event. She drove the kids to school and then set about doing her morning errands, making calls as she leap-frogged from the grocery store to the bank to the dry cleaners'. One of the places about which she inquired was Cleveland State University's Convocation Center, an arena where NCAA sporting competitions, concerts, and civic events are held. Pulling up to the dry cleaners' and parking just outside the double doors, Kathy was informed that renting the 14,000-seat facility would cost $18,000.

"Eighteen thousand dollars!" she exclaimed, stunned. She said thank you to the person at the other end and clicked END on her phone.

"Where are we ever going to get that kind of money?" she thought. She put her head down on the steering wheel and fought back tears.

Just then her phone rang. She glanced down at her caller ID and saw that Sam Lucarelli was calling.

Some months earlier Kathy had received a call from Sam's sister, Bernadette McClain, a former patient who had received a healing of cancer. Bernadette was calling Kathy on behalf of Sam's wife, Linda Lucarelli, who had suffered a massive heart attack while standing in line waiting to buy tickets at a movie theater.

Witnesses thought Linda had merely fainted, so precious minutes lapsed before emergency medical technicians were summoned. Unfortunately, the teenage theater workers were not certified to administer CPR. Attending paramedics commented that CPR probably would have made all the difference to the fifty-one-year-old's condition. By the time Linda was tended to by paramedics and arrived at the hospital, the damage was catastrophic. Although she was technically alive, Linda would never again live a normal day. She was, to put it bluntly, in a vegetative state.

Sam was inconsolable. Linda's father was nearly insensible with grief. When they married, Linda, who was childless, drew Sam's family into her heart as if they were her own children and grandchildren, and they missed her tremendously. And her friends were shocked. Linda—so pretty, so vibrant—Linda on life support? How could this be?

Sam moved Linda to St. Augustine Manor, a Catholic

long-term-care facility. He went to see her every day, as did her father. He wrote her notes and brought her cards. He fixed up Linda's room and made it as pretty as he could, bringing in Linda's bed linens and some furniture from home. He made certain there were fresh flowers in the room. He scattered family photographs all around. Sam placed Linda's cardigan sweaters around her shoulders so that she would feel more dressed. Linda's two best friends came every Saturday and gave her a pedicure, chatting and coaxing her to come out of her trance. Sometimes Linda opened her eyes and everyone would get wildly hopeful. But there was absolutely no responsiveness in those blue eyes that were once so bright and friendly.

Amidst this hopelessness, Bernadette called Kathy. "We can't bring Linda to you, Kathy. She's too sick. It's too hard to move her. Would you come to St. Augustine's and pray over her?" Of course Kathy went.

It is not unusual for Kathy to answer requests like Bernadette's. Whenever anyone asked her to come and pray, she'd buzz around to the Cleveland Clinic or University Hospitals after dropping the kids off at school. This was a side of Kathy few people saw. It was a little more unusual for Dr. Nemeh to make hospital calls because he was tied to the office six days a week, but he also went to Linda's bedside to pray over her.

"We always hope and pray that God will come through for each and every person," Kathy recalled of the visits she and Issam made to St. Augustine Manor. "But sometimes . . . sometimes it seems pretty obvious that God has other plans. And it was fairly clear that the Lord had other plans for Linda."

————

On a bleak day in March when Kathy was struggling to resolve the problem of the April 3 healing service and where to hold it, Sam just happened to call. He wanted to talk about Linda. When Sam heard Kathy's voice he knew her well enough to perceive something was wrong. He insisted she tell him what had her so worried, and the whole story came out.

Sam didn't think twice. "The one person who gave me hope in my despair was Dr. Nemeh," he told Kathy, "and I want others to know that hope. Kathy, let me pay for it. We'll do this in honor of Linda."

During the two weeks between Palm Sunday and the healing service held at Cleveland State University, Kathy, along with Patrick Coleman and other volunteers, focused on recruiting more help and on dispensing tickets. Kathy installed a dedicated telephone line at the office with a recording giving instructions on how people might obtain tickets. She also opened a post office box, so that when Cleveland's WEWS News Channel 5's lead anchor Ted Henry continued his coverage of the Nemeh story he was able to tell viewers they could send a self-addressed, stamped envelope to the P.O. box and tickets would be mailed back to them. Kathy, Carmie, Tia, and Patrick spent hours up at Dr. Nemeh's office stuffing envelopes with tickets. Sam helped by arranging for his staff to dispense tickets at his business in downtown Cleveland.

Kathy, Father Welsh, and Patrick visited the CSU Convocation Center, where the priest studied how they could situate an altar for the celebration of the Mass. There was an on-site meeting for all volunteers the night before the event. Patrick had sent around sign-up sheets and was gratified to see more than a hundred names on his volunteer list. He took home the lists and the arena seating charts. He would wrestle much of the night with how best to strategically place everyone around the facility.

Sunday, April 3, 2005, dawned clear and temperatures reached a high in the low fifties. It was like having good weather on election day: the mild weather helped the very sick and those caring for them to make their way from the suburbs to downtown Cleveland with a lot less trouble. It was quite a contrast from the weather on March 13, when nasty snow flurries were scattered about by knifelike winds.

And the people came. Based on collected tickets and an arena that was half full at its peak, an estimated seven thousand people attended.

Dr. Nemeh began praying at seven in the morning. At eleven Father Robert Welsh celebrated a Catholic Mass, and Sam and his entire family were seated by Linda's wheelchair in the center of the arena. It had taken an incredible effort on the part of many people to prepare Linda for this outing, but she was there dressed in white and ensconced in her wheelchair.

"She looks like an angel, doesn't she?" Sam commented as his sons and daughters, grandchildren, and friends—in all, about fifty people—gathered around. Frail, tiny, a bouquet of flowers resting on her lap, Linda was a heartbreaking sight. A little boy named Sam, the first grandson, carried Linda's flowers over to a statue of Blessed Mother and laid them at her feet. Few eyes were dry.

After Mass Dr. Nemeh and Kathy approached Linda. The call went out to everyone in attendance to extend their hands toward Linda and pray for her. Everyone was still. The feeling in the room was powerful. For ten minutes, seven thousand silent people released their prayers for Linda and their hopes for themselves into the care of the heavens—as if each prayer was an invisible messenger bird.

The Lucarelli family stayed two hours just meditating in the incredible spirit of the place. Finally Sam rose to leave. He pushed Linda's wheelchair across the floor toward the exit. Although he was being discreet and thought only to slip outside unobtrusively, the crowd noticed. Everyone who was able to stand rose to his or her feet in a thunderous ovation that lasted until Sam and Linda had disappeared behind the door.

The volunteers had planned to do what they could to make the long hours more tolerable with inspirational performances. Ashley Nemeh sang hymns. Volunteers recited the rosary. Patrick, a veteran piper, paused in his work to change into his bagpiper's uniform. Wearing the Mitchell tartan and standing on the second level just behind the draperies that separate the interior concourse from the brightly lit perimeter of the building, he started his bagpipes. People heard the ethereal strains of "Amazing Grace" from far away and up above until Patrick pushed through the curtains and slow-stepped to the railing, allowing the full volume of the beloved melody to fill the enormous complex.

Pretty, dark-haired mother of three Kim Toranto was very moved by Patrick's solo performance. She would wait more than fourteen hours for her prayer. A form of macular dystrophy called Stargardt's disease had robbed her of most of her vision. Her central vision was completely gone. Her corrected peripheral vision was 20/200 and 20/400. She could see, but it was not normal vision, not by any means. More than anything, Kim wanted to be able to see all three of her children at the same time.

Finally, she received her prayer from Dr. Nemeh. The next day, when her children were assembled in the kitchen before they went off to school, Kim realized she was able to see all of their faces at once for the first time. She burst out crying.

"Mommy, Mommy, why are you crying?" they asked, a chorus of confusion.

"Remember when Mommy went to 'church' all day and prayed?" she said through her tears. "Well, my prayers were answered! I can see you."

Kim contacted the Nemehs after her healing and described her joy at being able to see her children's eyelashes, the curve of their cheeks, and their smiles. She said she would never get over the thrill of being able to do simple things, like make peanut butter and jelly sandwiches for her children. Today, Kim sees in ways she never saw before—she sees extraordinary beauty and blessings in ordinary moments.

Mary Kay DeLong, who had been a Nemeh volunteer for a few months, asked her neighbor Don DeWitt if he would help just this once at the event at the Convocation Center at Cleveland State University. Good-naturedly, Don agreed, never dreaming this day would change his life.

His various duties included talking to people and helping them get where they needed to be. The arena was hard to maneuver for the really sick as well as for those pushing wheelchairs. He was busy all day. As he worked, he pondered the many varieties of sick people he encountered, and he felt a sense of awe at the great dignity with which these people conducted themselves. He was aware of feeling waves of compassion wash over him throughout the day. He was thinking everyone had come for a physical healing.

After having watched Dr. Nemeh praying for more than sixteen hours, just a few minutes before the clock struck twelve Don looked at the last circle of people over whom Dr. Nemeh would pray. In a moment of clarity, he realized that people are drawn to Dr. Nemeh by more than just the physical healings. Something inside Don was deeply touched by that knowledge. *To see so many people come for a ray of hope,* thought Don, a little stunned at the enormity of what had happened during the day.

Shortly thereafter he made up his mind he wanted to be part of this ministry.

"People can find the hope they're looking for here," he said of Dr. Nemeh's healing services.

Everyone connected with the Nemeh prayer ministry had to be out of CSU's Convocation Center by midnight so that the staff could begin to ready the arena for the next day's special event: the circus. At midnight, circus personnel had arrived and were beginning to unload equipment from eighteen-wheelers parked along Carnegie Avenue in single file, like elephants in parade, each one close behind another.

The Nemehs and their children, Fadia, Ashley, Debbie, and Wadi, along with Philip, Patrick, and the last of the volunteers, walked through the glass doors of the Cleveland State University Convocation Center into the clear night air and closed the book on a remarkable chapter of the Nemeh public prayer ministry. Issam had answered the call. It was his prayers and his hands that had drawn people to be where he was. It was his connection they sought. With impeccable patience, he had delivered a prayer to each one.

Thinking about the remarkable way that everybody was mollified once they received their prayer, Patrick commented, "It's like being at Disney World. No matter how long you wait in line, there's nothing but smiles at the exit gates."

20.

❧

Nowhere They'd Rather Be

·

With the unfolding of the Nemeh public prayer ministry, men and women coming to Dr. Nemeh through a variety of pathways began to offer their services as volunteers. Some were patients first; some met the Nemehs at a healing service hosted by their own parish; others became volunteers after they received their own healing.

It takes many people moving in a coordinated effort to pull off a healing service. Women act as ushers and troubleshooters. The responsibility of catching belongs primarily to men. Depending on the event, a group of anywhere from two to ten men and women are kept busy at the welcome table. Philip Keller assists by telling people what to expect and by helping people tell their healing stories. At any given time the volunteer roster includes about twenty people. They wait for an e-mail telling them the healing service schedule and they show up at the appointed hour.

Don DeWitt thought he was helping out for one day only on April 3, 2005, at the Cleveland State University Convocation Center event. He attended the next healing service, at which he volunteered as a catcher, and then he just kept coming back. Dr. Nemeh's spirituality and purpose made a strong first impression on Don. From the start he could see that the doctor's faith inspired hope in people—and that impression was validated at each subsequent event. Don has rarely missed a healing service since his first one.

Don says Dr. Nemeh has had an ineffable effect on him. He says he acquired a new awareness of God from the doctor. "I think about God more often, I talk to Him more, and I have incorporated daily prayer into my life." He also says he likes what being around Dr. Nemeh does: "It makes me feel calmer and more patient." When he receives a prayer from Dr. Nemeh, Don says, "I am treated to a bottomless sensation of peace." Don sees the doctor as a conduit to the Holy Spirit and predicts, "What is going to spread from him and his prayers is *faith*."

Don loves the camaraderie of the team atmosphere in the Nemeh prayer ministry. "We share in the spirituality of these healing services and belief in God and the Holy Spirit. We also realize none of us is in charge; no one person is more important than the next, and no one is irreplaceable. I know this ministry is going on with or without me. No one here is bigger than the purpose for being here. Even so . . ." Don searches for the right words. "You feel special when you are here. When you're in the workplace, people work for a reward and that reward is money. They want recognition because that translates into money and privilege. But there are no levels here. Stratifications do not exist. It's not the same thing when you talk about spirituality and God. And the more healing services I attend, the more I want to attend."

———

Joe Zabka came to Dr. Nemeh for a treatment and attended a healing service not long after that appointment. At his first healing service, Joe says, "I got a 'trifecta prayer'—a prayer from Dr. Nemeh, Kathy, and Sister Monica all at once—and it changed my life. I was a fallen-away Catholic, meaning that I sometimes went to Mass, but I didn't get anything much out of it. I didn't even really pray back then."

At his first healing service Joe witnessed a woman rise from her wheelchair and walk for the first time in five years. Her leg muscles had atrophied and she walked haltingly and clumsily, but she walked. He also saw a teenage boy who exhibited a speech difficulty owing to a brain lesion. When Kathy prayed over the boy he fell forward on her. Afterward the boy was able to enunciate clearly when he spoke to his mother.

Joe asked Kathy if he could volunteer in some capacity, and he has been a member of the team ever since. In fact, Joe teaches parish volunteers new to healing services the art of catching. He says, "For me, the attraction to Dr. Nemeh and Kathy and what they do is not about the miracles I have witnessed. It's about the kind of people the Nemehs are."

Joe's days are spent in a Cleveland bank working as project lead, which means he gathers resources, tracks issues and problems, and manages new projects so that the idea men can see their proposals come to fruition. Joe has always been passionate about math. To him, math is puzzles, and he loves to solve them. He also gets great satisfaction from teaching. He combines the two by teaching mathematics at the University of Phoenix, Cleveland campus. He was selected faculty member of the year for the College of General and Professional Studies for 2003. Thus he is a natural for the task of teaching new catchers.

Joe says he almost cannot remember his life before he met Dr. Nemeh. He observes his former self with curiosity and contrasts it with his present self: "I never thought of God; now I do. I never read the Bible; now I do. Dr. Nemeh brought me back to the Church, just because of the kind of person he is. Dr. Nemeh saved my soul." It's as though Dr. Nemeh's touch instigated the spinning of a spiritual gyroscope inside Joe's soul. The doctor's strong faith was a catalyst that launched Joe's faith on its own path.

"Dr. Nemeh shows me that one man *can* change the world one person at a time," says Joe. "People are becoming more and more aware of his work, but he should be doing this full-time instead of working at the office. Colleges and universities need to invite him to their campuses. Even though there are all these miracles with Dr. Nemeh, the miracles don't make you have faith in God. Being around *him* does."

Philip Keller first became one of Dr. Nemeh's patients in January 2000, when he came to the doctor hoping for a healing of retinitis pigmentosa, a congenital degenerative condition that had rendered him legally blind. "Within the first five seconds of entering Dr. Nemeh's suite," Philip loves to recall, "I met a patient cured of multiple sclerosis, a condition she had suffered for twenty years. *Note to self*, I thought. *This guy has potential.*"

Regular visits to Dr. Nemeh have yielded many physical blessings for Philip. A worrisome heart arrhythmia disappeared; varicose veins were erased; the sunkenness about the eye sockets common to blind people was corrected and his face restored to its natural structure; and the progression of blindness has been stanched. But a complete healing of his vision has yet to occur.

At one treatment session four months after Philip first became a patient, Dr. Nemeh voiced a prediction that "thousands will come, and you will be the voice of a ministry." Philip was taken aback. *Ministry? What ministry?* he thought. There was no hint of a public prayer ministry in spring of 2000. Philip stored the comment in his memory. In the meantime he continued to listen, and he says of Dr. Nemeh, "I heard nothing less than the voice of God speaking though this soft-spoken, unassuming, obedient servant."

When the Nemehs conducted their first open-to-the-public healing service at St. Ignatius High School's St. Mary of the Assumption Chapel on Mother's Day 2001, Philip was convinced his vision would be restored on that day and in that place. "It just felt so special," he recalled. "We were in a real church, not a private chapel. The Mass was beautiful, and the prayers were being prayed in such a gorgeous, holy place." Dr. Nemeh placed Philip right at his side as he prayed over people. Philip shuffled along beside the doctor for hours. The day wore on, and when the last person had been prayed over there was still no change in Philip's vision.

"I was devastated when my own healing did not happen that day," Philip admitted. "At first I had a real hard time reconciling my faith with the fact that there was no miracle for me. I asked, 'Why didn't God include me?' And finally I came to the realization that I was just another of the doctor's patients. Admittedly, I'm closer than most to the doctor and Kathy, but in the final analysis I am simply another patient who will be healed in God's time. In *God's* time, not *mine*."

During the subsequent healing services held at St. Mary of the Assumption Chapel at St. Ignatius, Philip was unable to walk beside Dr. Nemeh as he prayed over people because the room was too crowded. Philip's vision proved too poor to navigate the close spaces. Keenly disappointed, he was forced to take a seat. Or, as he understood it a little later within the framework of what Philip calls his "Indiana Jones philosophy of religion . . . I got out of the way of the boulder. I got out of the way and let God's design take over."

It was precisely *because* he was no longer on the front line of Dr. Nemeh's prayers, precisely *because* he took a seat in a pew, that Philip became accessible to the people. They made their way to him, coming in a steady stream to tell Philip their healing stories. Philip listened carefully. When they seemed eager to share he asked, "Would you like to tell everyone your story?" Often, they did. Philip would introduce the person at the microphone up at the altar or at the pulpit, give a preamble, and then step aside while the story was related. People told Philip that when he shared his personal journey it was helpful and inspirational.

As far as not receiving the healing of his sight, Philip says he has come to understand that God wants to demonstrate something powerful with a miracle Philip feels sure is in his future. When it occurs, says Philip, everyone will understand why he had to wait. Even so, Philip insists that what is most important to him is the effect of Dr. Nemeh's faith on his own spirituality. Some years after they first met, Philip confessed to Issam, "I had been a 'fringe Catholic' for years, but when I met you I felt as though I had been ushered into weekly catechism lessons on the essence of love and healing. I have watched you and your family living the Bible in a way more potent and true than most people preach it."

Some volunteers, such as George Sangrik, were simply helping their parish host a healing service when they met Dr. Nemeh. George belongs to both St. Mary Church in Hudson, Ohio, and St. Barnabas Catholic Church in Northfield, Ohio. Because he likes to make a difference in the lives of people in need, volunteering in just one parish was not enough for George. When it was announced at a St. Barnabas parish meeting that the Nemeh team would be coming for a healing service, it was a given that George's name would be on the list of helpers.

His attitude before meeting Dr. Nemeh was, "I didn't believe it—at least not the dramatic and ego-filled 'miraculous healings' you typically see on television. I didn't disbelieve it either." When the day of the St. Barnabas healing service came, George attended the noon Mass preceding the healing service and then worked as a catcher until the event was over at one-thirty in the morning. George has been a catcher at almost every service since.

George Sangrik's career as a first-rate freelance nature photographer takes him to some of the most pristine, elegant, remote, untouched corners of the world. He could overbook himself with photography assignments if he were so inclined, but instead he schedules his work around the Nemeh healing service calendar. Although he can travel anywhere with ease and command the world with his lens, George gives priority to being in a quiet room catching dozens of people who fall in the Spirit after a prayer. Why? "As catchers, we are fortunate to see what is happening right up close and to be part of it. We couldn't possibly doubt. It's right here in front of us: proof there is a God."

Being a catcher fascinates George. "At first I was surprised by the unusual heat radiating from the people I caught. It's a different kind of heat, way too hot for normal body temperature." He also enjoys helping those in the prayer line who are feeling anxious. Sometimes while Dr. Nemeh prays his way around the room, George has time to listen as these people voice their fears. George responds with compassion.

Once in a while people will turn around to face George and inform him that his assistance will not be needed. "People don't believe it's going to happen to them," he says. "They tell me, 'You can go help someone else because I'm certainly not falling down on the floor.' I just smile and tell them I can't leave; I might get in trouble if I left my position, and they wouldn't want that for me."

Sharon DeSanto was one of those who told George she would not need his assistance. She came to a healing service because her husband asked her to accompany him. In January 2006, at the age of fifty-one, Emil DeSanto, who started his days at five every morning by reading his Bible, was diagnosed with a combination esophageal and stomach cancer. He consulted Dr. Nemeh, who treated him and foresaw a wonderful healing in his future; in fact, Dr. Nemeh's opinion was that

Emil would do better not to undergo surgery for the cancer. He loved his appointments with Dr. Nemeh, and told family and friends he thought Dr. Nemeh was as close to God as anyone he had ever met in his life. He felt spiritually empowered after spending time with Dr. Nemeh.

Nevertheless, Emil decided to abandon the sessions with Dr. Nemeh and focus instead on the course of treatment prescribed by his oncologists. Emil and Sharon believed at first that they were trying for a cure—they understood Emil's chances of beating the cancer to be 35 percent. They later learned from his doctors that after surgery there was only a 3 percent survival rate in other patients with Emil's type of cancer.

Emil underwent a week of chemotherapy followed by ten days of around-the-clock radiation. He rested a few weeks before surgery, which was performed on March 28, 2006. Afterward Emil was sustained by intravenous drip but was not permitted even a drop of water to pass his lips for twenty days. He dreamed of ginger ale and tall glasses of cold drinks. Post-surgical tests showed that the cancer was on a rampage; more chemotherapy and two more rounds of radiation followed. By this time he looked like a concentration camp victim.

Emil was thirty-five years old when he finally found the woman of his dreams, Sharon Boyle. When they married in 1989, Emil assumed two roles: husband, and stepfather to Sharon's adorable ten-year-old daughter, Tanya. He was thrilled to be a parent and doted on Tanya as her school years unfolded. Seventeen years later, as Emil struggled through the horrific assault on his body, Tanya was planning a June wedding. Emil's most powerful motivation to get better was the desire to be at her side as she walked down the aisle in her bridal gown.

The summer months seemed to be about regaining his strength, and everyone was hopeful Emil had beaten the odds. It was only an illusion. On November 30, 2006, Emil's oncologists predicted he had three months to live.

It was after receiving this news that Emil asked Sharon to take him to a healing service. Sharon did, although she was skeptical. "All these people falling down," she scoffed. "I find it hard to believe! Surely they must be faking." She told Emil she did not want to go up for a prayer.

Emil protested. "Sharon, Dr. Nemeh is a true man of God," he said. "He doesn't take any credit for any of this. If these people are passing out it is the Holy Spirit doing it to them. I am going up there for a prayer, and I wish you would come too. Besides, honey," he added, persuasively, "you've been through breast cancer. It wouldn't hurt to get a prayer. You will need strength as my caretaker and could use an additional blessing."

Sharon relented.

Standing in the prayer line beside her husband, she peeked around to get a closer look at the doctor. *He's so mild*, she thought, and he seemed to her to be a very kind person. He approached each individual with respect. He made eye contact with them and nodded in a wordless greeting just before he raised his hands and began murmuring his prayer. She studied his hands. There was no predicting whether he would touch people with his fingertips, or lay a palm gently over their hearts, or press both hands over other body parts such as their backs or knees; sometimes he simply pointed his fingers toward their eyes, ears, or throat.

As the doctor prayed his way toward them, Sharon turned

to the silver-haired gentleman standing behind her—her catcher—and told him, "You can go help someone else. I won't need your help. No way am I going to fall."

George Sangrik just smiled at Sharon. He shook his head no, and delivered his standard response: he was sure that she didn't want him to get in trouble for leaving his position. Sharon felt a little irritated at his presence, but she didn't argue.

She watched closely as Dr. Nemeh stepped in front of her husband. He smiled at this patient for whom he had developed great affection. Sharon was astonished when he barely touched Emil's forehead, whispered a word or two she couldn't hear, and then Emil was suddenly floating backward into the outstretched arms of his catcher.

Dr. Nemeh sidestepped over to Sharon and raised his hands. His lips moved in a nearly soundless prayer. After a few seconds of trying to hear what he was saying, everything went black; Sharon remembers nothing more until she opened her eyes and realized she was lying on the floor.

Emil and Sharon discussed Dr. Nemeh following this healing service experience. Emil expressed profound regret. "I *wish* I had listened to Dr. Nemeh," he told her. "I *should* have listened to him. If I had known him better—maybe if I had gone to him two or three times a week—then I would have understood. I would never have gone forward with that surgery. And I would not be dying."

By the time he came back to Dr. Nemeh in the fall of 2006, Emil's body was ravaged. Both Dr. Nemeh and Emil acknowledged that even though there are no limitations to God's healing powers, Emil would not get the full healing that had beckoned in the beginning. Emil told everyone he was okay with that. "Everyone has to die," he consoled Sharon when she cried and cried. "I wish I could live longer. But my time to go is now."

Emil resumed treatments with Dr. Nemeh for pain management. After each appointment Emil's pain diminished significantly. He was able to spend every day alert and fully participating because he did not need heavy pain medications. The only prescription he relied upon was a small dose of morphine at night to help him sleep. Moreover, Emil's spirituality received an infusion. These two gifts of healing helped sustain Emil through the last months of his life.

Hours before his death, Emil talked of Dr. Nemeh. "I love that man," he said, genuine warmth in his voice. "I think he is a disciple. A true holy man. I absolutely love him.

"I owe him so much," Emil continued. "I may not have gotten the miracle of a physical healing, but I did get a miracle: my miracle is that Dr. Nemeh took away my pain. I have been pain-free and almost drug-free. That, for me, is miracle enough."

Emil died with great dignity on February 25, 2007. He had told his family and friends he was ready to meet his Lord God. He confessed one regret: he would not live to be a grandfather to the children with whom Tanya, the beautiful bride he had been so proud to escort down the aisle, might be blessed.

Getting prayed over by Dr. Nemeh is, for George Sangrik, an unparalleled experience.

"I always take a lot of prayers with me into the healing session. I bring a list of other people I'm praying for. Usually I bring a picture of someone too.

"I caught so many people before I went down in the Spirit. I have no idea what kind of faller I am, but it seems to me that

I am floating. And I am totally, totally at peace. I could be in the mountains, I could be anywhere in the world, and what happens here—well, I can't think of anything more beautiful than when you are prayed over. It just blows that other stuff all away. Dr. Nemeh brought the Holy Spirit into my life. The Spirit is active, accessible, present and accounted for in my life. Dr. Nemeh also brought me closer to God."

Watching Dr. Nemeh work at close proximity, George gets an intimate view of personal moments others don't get a chance to observe. In their intense fright, people talk. And when they are eye to eye, people sometimes ask: *Dr. Nemeh, am I going to die?*

"Sometimes the doc looks sad," George says. "You don't know what he knows." Pause. "You don't *want* to know."

Those who volunteer for the Nemehs bring their own unique stories into the mix. Tricia Kaman, the portrait artist who had come to Sts. Peter and Paul on March 13, 2005, benefited in so many ways from Dr. Nemeh's care and prayers that she continued regular, preventive health care treatments with him. In the course of coming to know and love the doctor, she, too, was moved to join the Nemehs' prayer ministry as a volunteer. She created the logo that depicts Dr. Nemeh's long-held vision of the "Path to Faith."

Charlene Kalo, pastry chef and caterer, became a volunteer when her relationship with her customer Kathy Nemeh morphed from client to friend. Like George, who makes his schedule around the healing services, Charlene found it easy to decide what to do when conflicts arose. Each time she helped at a service, Charlene felt as if she were playing a role, small though it might be, in accomplishing God's work. She explained the reasoning behind deciding between a personal commitment and helping at a healing service: "How could I say 'no' to God?" she asks with a smile. "How could I say 'no' to serving Him?"

Charlene invited a friend, Karen David, to a healing service. Overwhelmed by the faith of the people in attendance as well as the simple, humble expressions of love and patience emanating from Dr. Nemeh, Karen found herself weeks later becoming not only a patient but also a volunteer. "Dr. Nemeh is a strong instrument working in partnership with the Creator," she says. "God sends the energy by means of the Holy Spirit through Issam, and he gets himself totally out of the way. He is similar to a living saint."

In May 2006 electronics engineer Dennis Sedlak answered a call from his home parish, St. Joseph Byzantine Catholic Church in Brecksville, for volunteers to help at a larger gathering to be held in St. John the Baptist Cathedral in Parma, which is the nerve center for Byzantine churches in the eastern United States. "I had no idea who this Dr. Nemeh was," says Dennis. "It didn't matter. I volunteered to be a catcher . . . whatever *that* was!"

His wife planned to join him later in the afternoon, but he telephoned her early on, saying, "Rose Marie, you have to get here. This is unbelievable. It's like being in heaven! I can't explain it. You just have to come."

After one prayer, both husband and wife were blown away. When they recovered from having fallen in the Spirit, they looked at each other and knew. "I'm going to see if Dr. Nemeh needs any help," Rose Marie said. She asked around and was directed to Kathy. She recognized Kathy Ghazoul Nemeh right away; they had known each other in their teen years. "Do you need any help?" she asked Kathy. "My husband and I would love to volunteer." Kathy immediately invited Rose Marie and Dennis to join them at the dinner break.

"With that first healing service, my life changed," says Rose Marie, an educator consultant. "Dennis and I were walking on a cloud. We found something in the Nemehs' public prayer ministry that we can both share, something we can give our time and talents to. Now, we arrange our vacations, weekends, and commitments around the healing service calendars. If we could do this full-time we would."

Throughout the years of volunteering, the Sedlaks have been blessed with various healings. Dennis was able to cancel surgery to correct a diagnosed rotator cuff injury. "With one treatment the pain went away," Dennis says. "Dr. Nemeh told me it was actually pinched nerves." Also, in February 2008 Dennis underwent the insertion of three stents; in May he failed the follow-up stress test. Dr. Nemeh prayed over him because his coloring looked off, and he told Dennis that "he had received a healing." This was a curious statement considering all the heart work that he had undergone. When the cardiologist put in another stent, he discovered that an artery had been nicked when one of the original stents had been inserted. The nicked artery should have caused a heart attack. Thus, when Dr. Nemeh told Dennis he had received a healing, he was right.

Volunteer Maureen Leimkuehler introduced her son, Bill, an engineer, to Dr. Nemeh in the spring of 2007. All seventeen years of Bill's education had taken place in Catholic institutions. Bill describes his mind as being highly logical, methodical, and analytical, and he admits that he has struggled for years with how to reconcile the seemingly disparate worlds of faith and science.

He remembers: "When I met Dr. Nemeh, he explained the details of the connection between healings and the science of those healings. For the first time, I could see a world in which previously unexplainable phenomena such as miraculous healings could be explained through both faith and science simultaneously. It felt as though a key piece to the puzzle of my life had been given to me."

Since then, Bill has spent hundreds of hours shadowing the doctor, filming public appearances and private prayer work. Dr. Nemeh and Bill are working together on various projects, one of which is to produce a documentary that will illustrate the connection between science and spirituality. Bill has witnessed many amazing healings and miracles in the course of this project, but for him the most memorable of all moments was that first meeting with Dr. Nemeh.

"Dr. Nemeh is a man after God's own heart," Bill says. "He dedicates his life to serving the Lord, doing His will every day. Because of his commitment to God he has the wisdom that comes with belonging to God, and therefore can share the answers to long-standing questions many people are afraid to ask themselves."

Nancy Inch, healing service coordinator since the latter half of 2006, was led to volunteer for the Nemehs because of her husband's journey through glioblastoma multiforme, the most aggressive kind of primary brain tumor, which is nearly

always terminal. On March 28, 2002, Bill Inch suffered a seizure while driving and, as a result, was involved in a terrible car
accident. The air bag deployed in such a way that Bill sustained
seven fractures in his face. A brain scan revealed that the reason
for the seizure was this previously unsuspected brain tumor.
The prognosis given Bill was that he would live, at most, another eight to twelve weeks.

Bill was told by neurologists at the Cleveland Clinic and at
the Tisch Brain Tumor Center at Duke University that there
was nothing that could be done to help him. Nancy refused to
accept that no one could help her husband, so she searched the
Cleveland Yellow Pages for an acupuncturist and chose Dr. Issam Nemeh. She says he was the right choice. Bill lived twenty-
two more months, time that was crucial to Nancy's well-being
because it allowed her time to accept that Bill was being called
"home" to be with God.

"Dr. Nemeh gave us hope," says Nancy. "He gave us the
ability to have joy every day. Bill had a standing appointment
every Friday for ten months, and we attended all the healing
services during that period of time. Through Dr. Nemeh's in-
tercession, God gave Bill and me numerous healings. I know
God gave me the strength to care for Bill, because when I look
back, I have no idea how I was able to do it for twenty-two
months without help.

"Treatments from Dr. Nemeh straightened Bill's broken,
crooked nose so that he could once again breathe normally,"
said Nancy. The broken eye sockets had caused Bill to lose his
peripheral vision, but this, too, was restored. Bill had a hernia so serious it kept him from serving in the military during the Vietnam War; when Bill became wheelchair bound,
he complained about how much it hurt. The doctor prayed

over Bill and the next morning the hernia that had been there for thirty-five years was gone. Dr. Nemeh and Bill developed a warm friendship during this time, and when it became difficult for Bill to speak, Dr. Nemeh was somehow able to understand his thoughts and communicate them to his family, for which Bill was grateful.

By January 5, 2004, Nancy was beginning to understand that it was Bill's time to go, that he was staying alive until she was able to gracefully relinquish her husband to God's heavenly care.

From a young age, Issam Nemeh displayed a knack for languages. He is fluent in Arabic, Aramaic, Polish, French, German, and, of course, English. He also understands enough Bulgarian, Romanian, and Serbian to be able to communicate with patients who speak these languages. But many patients report he is gifted in another type of language: the unspoken language of the heart. This gift would become apparent in the final hours of Bill's life.

Two weeks after Bill's final brain scan, Bill's breathing became so labored that Nancy called Dr. Nemeh in a panic. He was at their house in five minutes. He checked his patient and "talked" with him, even though Bill was unable to verbalize what he was thinking. Dr. Nemeh then told Nancy, "He's dehydrated. We should get him to the nursing home." Bill was transported to a nursing care facility and was tucked into bed by three in the morning. Later, Dr. Nemeh confessed to Nancy, "He 'told' me I had to get him out of the house. He didn't want to die in his hospital bed in your family room; he knew it would be too painful for you, and he wanted to spare you that memory."

Hours later, on January 24, Nancy finally arrived at the

emotional destination Bill's journey had been taking her all along. She realized her husband had suffered enough. She gathered Bill up in her arms and whispered in his ear, "It's time for you to go with God now." Bill died the very next instant after Nancy uttered those words.

Nancy continued attending the healing services after her husband passed away. Mostly, she sat in the back of the church saying prayers and crying. Her first active role in the healing services was to help on the Day of the Ten Thousand. Now, as a way of giving back, she performs a myriad of tasks that help make the Nemeh public prayer ministry run smoothly. "Bill always said, 'When I get better, I want to help Dr. Nemeh in any way I can.' Well, Bill can't, so I work in his place. I feel great compassion for those coming to the healing services hoping for a miracle because I have been there."

As team leader, Nancy keeps volunteers notified of upcoming events and announcements concerning the prayer ministry. Once Dr. Nemeh and Kathy accept an invitation to conduct a healing service at a church or other facility, a great deal of the responsibility of ensuring that the day proceeds as it should is turned over to Nancy. She visits the site to determine where the prayers will take place and how the room will be set up. She divides the day into time slots, allocates tickets within those slots, and has the tickets printed and dispensed. She forwards a handbook to the parish coordinators and stays in contact with them to answer their questions.

"Dr. Nemeh is hope, love, patience, and compassion," says Nancy. "We should all try to follow his example."

What all the Nemeh team volunteers seem to share is an abiding respect for Dr. Nemeh and Kathy, deep pride in being part of this prayer ministry, and a conviction that what they are doing for the public prayer ministry is in God's name and for His greater glory.

At each healing service it is as if God is parading His limitless creativity. And even as joy floats like an invisible balloon, a gigantic sadness also hangs heavy in the air. For there is ample evidence of the infinite ways that human beings can go awry.

Nevertheless, the volunteers agree there is nowhere else they would rather be.

21

Chevron Flight

An inverted V scoots across a flannel gray sky. Honks pierce the frosty chill and then flutter down to deciduous forests. Busy and purposeful, the geese know when to lead and when to trade off in rotations performed seamlessly, with one now dropping behind and another surging forward to fill the gap. Their winged choreography is to the sky what synchronized swimming is to a pool.

The word "chevron" derives from the Latin word for goat: *caper*. In its plural form, *caprioli*, it assumes a different connotation, referring to the point at which two pieces of wood meet. Another derivation comes from the Old French word *chevre*, meaning "rafter." When two beams of wood meet at the apex, as with rafters in a roof, they form a symbolic resemblance to the horns of a butting goat. Chevron is also the Hebrew biblical name of a Levite and a variant of the Hebrew word *chever*, or, "association." So the concept that underlies the essence of "chevron" is meeting, coming together, and being in association with one another.

Like those geese flying their inverted V in that moody October sky.

Like the volunteers at a Nemeh healing service.

As they proceeded from the memorable, enormous healing services held in March of 2005, the Nemeh team figured out how better to help the people who came for prayer. They initiated a new system of pacing the healing services with timed vouchers so that everyone didn't arrive at the beginning of the service and have to wait an interminable length of time for a prayer.

They learned that people could bring photographs of their loved ones and that when Dr. Nemeh pointed his fingers at the pictures and prayed over them, healings happened.

Sometimes people would tell Kathy of a loved one who could not attend the service. "Just hold the image of your loved one in your heart," she always advised. A flood of grateful notes and happy e-mails described the fruitfulness of these prayers in absentia. At Church on the Rise in Westlake, a mother put her estranged son's image in her mind and prayed that their relationship would somehow be mended. After she had received her prayer, she sat in a chair crying. Her cell phone vibrated. It was her son. They talked for the first time in years.

At Immaculate Heart of Mary Church in Cuyahoga Falls, the Nemeh volunteers learned that animals are healed too. At 9:30 that evening, the pastor, Father Tom McCann, carried his tumor-ridden dog, Joy, into the church. After Issam extended his hands and prayed, the animal visibly relaxed in Father McCann's arms. The next day Patrick made a follow-up call to the rectory for feedback and constructive criticism. Father McCann wasn't in, so Patrick left a message. A jubilant Father McCann telephoned Patrick later in the evening. "I just got back from the veterinarian. Joy's tumors are all benign."

Every service is as unique as the needs, hopes, and wishes of the individuals who attend. The tempos are different; the vibes have different resonances. Sometimes there is a palpable charge in the air, as on a day in 2006 at St. Bernadette's Church, when Kathy felt a strong calling to interrupt Issam's methodical progression through the line of people awaiting a prayer. She didn't know why she touched him on the sleeve. She didn't even really know where she was going to lead him. She pulled Issam from the far left side of the altar to the other side of the church. She found herself halting before a wheelchair-bound woman who was parked on the far right side of the altar.

A little more than a year earlier, this woman, Veronica Lowney, was a newlywed when she climbed a six-foot ladder to put some wedding presents into storage. Her dog ran under the ladder, causing Veronica to tumble to the ground. Her spinal column was fractured when she hit the floor and she was paralyzed. She was told she would never walk again.

Dr. Nemeh extended his hands and began praying over Veronica. Chris Krysniak, seated three pews back, recalled feeling a swirling, pulsating intensity. She says she sensed a strange and powerful change in the energy. She began to cry because, she says, "I was overwhelmed. I knew, and everyone in that church knew, we were going to witness a miracle. I heard Dr. Nemeh telling the woman, 'You are getting the healing. It will be all right. You can get up.'"

Veronica looked to Kathy in her fright; Kathy extended her arms outward and encouraged her, saying, "Just come to me. You will be okay."

Dr. Nemeh continued to pray. With kindness in his voice, he urged her, "Get up, get up. You will be able to walk."

At three o'clock Veronica Lowney rose from her wheelchair and walked.

Veronica was able to climb the altar steps and tell her story to those in the church, most of whom were crying after having witnessed her miracle. Veronica mentioned that she was anxious to go to her parents' home, where she was expected for Sunday dinner. She couldn't wait to surprise her father, who had been devastated by his daughter's paralysis, by walking in the front door on her own two feet.

Kathy watched as Veronica and her husband walked down the aisle and out St. Bernadette's doors. Veronica had entered this church seated in a wheelchair, but when she left, she was pushing the wheelchair she would never need again in front of her.

Many people come to one of the healing services for a prayer and stay, just steeping in the prayerful atmosphere for hours. Some take advantage of the serene environment to sort out their lives. Those who sit for a while find that they can perceive a rhythm in the prayer work. The catchers, the ushers, the Nemehs; what they do looks like a choreographed ballet wherein the dance is driven by the stories behind the characters. Priests, pastors, church volunteers, and team members become swirling curlicues of motion amidst the drama of physical, spiritual, and emotional healings. There is an aura of spotlight shining down on the two principals, Dr. Nemeh and Kathy. All eyes are on them as they glide smoothly, now together, now apart. The only element missing in this spiritual ballet is the curtain call. There are no bows taken, ever, by either the doctor or his wife. The applause is all for God.

22

Renaissance of Faith

Church communities frequently view Dr. Nemeh's prayer ministry as a grassroots phenomenon that invariably brings out the best in parishioners. Volunteers work long hours preparing for the event. Hospitality committees rally parishioners to donate baked goods, and refreshments are usually served all day long. Greeters are posted at the doors and attendants in the parking lots. After the event, when testimonials and feedback are gathered, many pastors and clergy notice a resurgence in parish life. One person at a time, and one congregation at a time, Dr. Nemeh's prayers are inspiring a renaissance of faith.

Father Daniel Schlegel is a priest who understands the impact of Dr. Nemeh's healing services. The Nemehs held services at the Church of the Holy Angels in Bainbridge four times in the first six years that Father Dan was pastor, from 2003 through 2008. Father Dan is impressed by what he has seen. "Issam Nemeh would say that he is nothing special," Father Dan says. "But I think he is a holy man. He is a conduit to God through whom grace flows in a special way."

When he met Dr. Nemeh, Father Dan was amazed at the doctor's humility. "There's something about him in that it's *not* about him. The aura around him is . . . different. His humility is something people can relate to—that 'I'm nothing special' attitude." Father Dan reminisces about the first healing service during which thirteen hundred people received a prayer from Issam. "Someone administered full-time all that summer just taking requests for tickets. The hardest thing was dealing with the desperation. So many were so sick."

Father Dan, like Father Fata, made it a point to anoint churchgoers throughout the day. "Anointing with oil is so powerful," he says. "Oil has the ability to bind things together. When you are praying over people and anointing, you're binding them to the prayers of the Church.

"The response to the first healing service was overwhelming. When an immediate healing is not granted, people are naturally disappointed. With Issam, it doesn't matter. They may not receive the gift they came for or thought they were searching for, but they get what God has in mind for them. Sometimes a healing is just freeing the spirit that holds us bound to a trauma."

Father Dan is grateful to the Nemehs for reviving his parish. "My parish has been forever changed. The numbers are up, that's for sure, but it's more about the depth of faith people have. My parishioners told me, 'We have been born again in the Spirit. This is no longer a faith that is outside of me.' And the most moving part of hosting a healing service isn't even the day of the service. It's the follow-up meeting afterward. Testimony after testimony is given."

He lists the experiences of some of his parishioners in a run-on recapitulation of some highlights. "One mother came with her Down's syndrome daughter. She had been at a loss, completely unsure what God wanted from her and her husband. She got a prayer and fell in the Spirit. Her little girl clung to her as she lay resting in the Spirit. The Spirit washed away all this mother's doubt, fear, and confusion. When she awoke she knew what God's plan was and felt contented that she could handle anything that came her way.

"Brian came with his wife, only in support of her wish to receive a prayer. He was not going to get a prayer, no way, no how. He gets here and says, 'What the heck.' For three years he had been unable to turn his head—his neck mobility was nearly zero. They got into the car that night and his wife said to him, 'Brian, do you realize what you're doing? You're turning your head.' He could look all around again, just like normal.

"Joe, battling cancer, came and was not impressed. But he didn't stay and he didn't get prayed over. I tried to tell him, 'Joe, I disagree with you.' Conversion happens on different levels . . ." Here the priest shakes his head with regret, or sadness, or a combination of both, thinking of Joe, the one who got away.

"Mary Frank: her breast cancer vanished.

"Rebecca Lawes: a powerful story. She was on vacation, forgot the doctor was coming, and when she remembered at the last minute, she and her husband dragged all three children to the church in their pajamas. With Dr. Nemeh's prayer, God reached into her heart and took out all her bitterness and anger, and for the first time in years she was able to feel love for people who had hurt her. Her husband had suffered three brain aneurysms; after he received his prayer they never recurred.'

"This is truly a health and wellness ministry."

———

For three hours on the day of the Nemeh healing service, parishioner Mary Frank directed traffic in the Church of the Holy Angels parking lot. As people left the church and were walking to their cars, she conducted an informal poll. She asked, "What did you think?" Nearly everyone had the same reaction. They shook their heads and said, quite simply, "Wow." Right before her volunteer shift was over she queried a couple as they emerged from the church. "Are you parishioners? What did you think?"

"We are not members but our son Danny is here," they answered. Seeing Mary's confusion, the lady clarified: "Do you know Father Dan? He is our son."

Mary entered the church thinking about the powerful implications of her parish priest so believing in this Dr. Nemeh that he made certain his own parents came to receive a prayer.

Mary sat in the church for several hours, absorbing the peaceful atmosphere and saying prayers. Just four days earlier she had been diagnosed with breast cancer. That evening, she told her husband, Don, and two sons, Daniel and David, the dreadful news. Theirs was a strong but quiet faith, and the men hovered, respecting her internal struggle and fear but anxious to express their concern and love. David slipped out of the house and returned shortly afterward with a pink cancer bracelet for each member of the family. Everything was happening so fast. She was scheduled for surgery but she didn't know what to expect—lumpectomy, mastectomy, surgical removal of lymph nodes? It was a scary blur. She and Don attended a wedding that weekend and Mary cried the entire time, thinking, *I'll never see my boys be married!*

After meditating for quite some time at the Church of the Holy Angels, Mary finally stepped up to the prayer line for her prayer. Dr. Nemeh barely reached out to her and she fell in the Spirit. She felt warmth and peace. Time, for Mary, did not exist. She was aware only of peace and that warm blanket of Love that conveyed a message that everything would be fine. She knew for sure that God would take care of her.

"The next day," Mary says, "the impossible happened. The Cleveland Clinic called, saying there had been a cancellation and their state-of-the-art MRI, booked solid for months in advance, was suddenly available. Could I come right in for a surgical ultrasound? I did. And I reassured everyone, 'Whatever you have to do is fine. God is with me.'"

Her husband joined her in the recovery room, where the surgeon told the couple, "We don't know what happened. It wasn't what we thought it was going to be." The cells were sent to three hospital laboratories where tests were performed nine times because there was no consensus among the doctors on what they were viewing.

Mary was the least confused of everyone. "I know what happened," says Mary. "Through Dr. Nemeh, God healed me. God's presence was there at that healing service." Years later Mary Frank still cannot talk about Issam Nemeh without crying. "Dr. Nemeh was sent to us to help us know of God's presence. Because of Dr. Nemeh, we know that God is among us."

Rebecca Lawes brought a lifetime of hurt to the prayer line at Holy Angels. Her adoptive parents had destroyed her childhood with constant emotional and physical abuse. As a result she suffered from bitterness and debilitating memories.

Even so, she says, she did not allow the ugly abuse to poison her faith in God.

When Dr. Nemeh approached her she was surprised to hear herself blurt out, "I have cancer of the soul." When the doctor prayed over her, Rebecca fell in the Spirit. She says a vision of a brilliant white light came to her and she was given a message: "Your faith has healed you." Her husband, Philip, and two of her three daughters, Lindsey and Lauren, also fell in the Spirit.

After everyone had been prayed over, Rebecca's family retreated to a pew in the back of the church. At twelve-thirty that night, while her youngest daughter Erin chattered away, happily immured in her four-year-old resilience, the rest of the family struggled to recuperate from their prayers. Lindsey didn't want to leave. She kept repeating, "Mommy, this is where I belong. He came to me and told me, 'This is where you belong.'" Lauren kept repeating that Christ was with her. Philip knew definitively that he had seen Christ. They stayed until the church closed at ten minutes to one.

"Our entire family was very affected," Rebecca told Father Dan. "For eleven days my daughter Lauren told me that Christ was walking with her; she could feel Him. 'He's right here,' she said. 'He's walking with me, Mom.' Lauren had always had a constellation of issues, elusive things that made her seem different. During the next couple of weeks there were no issues. Sometime later she was diagnosed with autism, which provided a helpful framework for understanding some of her behaviors, but after Dr. Nemeh prayed over her, she enjoyed a sustained interlude of calm."

Rebecca said, "My husband watched his thirty-five-year-old father die of antithrombin III deficiency [ATIII], a blood disorder that is characterized by clots forming in veins and arteries. Philip was only twelve years old when his father developed a fatal blood clot in the back of his neck. At the time of the healing service, Philip had one hundred percent of his right sinus filled and nearly one hundred percent of the left sinus filled, and he was flirting with death. When he went to see his medical specialist after having attended the service, the clot had vanished.

"As for me," Rebecca continued, "it was a life-changing experience." She told her pastor she needed Dr. Nemeh to open the door to the forgiveness and peace that had eluded her.

Issam and Father Dan have come to know each other very well in the years since that first healing service. Issam regards Father Dan with ineffable respect and says of him, "He is a true priest."

Father Dan states, "Issam Nemeh is a holy man. God's grace flows through him. He delivers God's impassioned Love in newly recognizable forms and expressions. People relate to him because of his sincere humility, because it makes him approachable and real. I think people are so longing to be connected to God, and Dr. Nemeh sees that. He helps them connect."

In March 2005 Bishop Roger W. Gries was asked by Father Ted Marszal to assist at the Sts. Peter and Paul healing service, and so he was on scene for the Day of the Ten Thousand to witness what happens when Issam prays.

Bishop Gries says, "I think Issam is a person who was called by Jesus, and he has said yes to that call, and he has followed Jesus. He is using the gifts that God gave him to carry on the work that Jesus has given him. Some of this work is with prayers and some is with medicine. Issam is using the medicine to support the work that Jesus has called him to do. I believe in what Issam is doing. Issam Nemeh is a comrade—a fellow worker in the vineyard."

Bishop Gries was born and raised in Cleveland. He graduated with honors from Benedictine High School, where he returned to teach, coach, and serve as principal after having attained his bachelor's and master's degrees. In 1957 he took his vows as a monk of St. Andrew Abbey, a Roman Catholic Benedictine monastery, and later served as abbot there.

Father Gries was named Auxiliary Bishop of Cleveland and Titular Bishop of Praesidium in 2001 and has endeared himself to Clevelanders in that capacity ever since. He is a captivating speaker, and is as approachable and as good a listener as Santa Claus. He has earned an impeccable reputation within the religious community.

Bishop Roger has come to know the Nemehs better since that cold March day in 2005, and he has a high regard for both of them.

"Mrs. Nemeh is a wonderful woman. She is the ministry spokesperson and a fabulous speaker. The first time I heard her tell her story she brought fifteen hundred three-by-five cards up to the podium." He chuckles. "But it was a very good talk."

In describing Issam's calling, the bishop says, "Jesus told His apostles to go out and heal. 'The flock is great but the shepherds are few.' Since Vatican II, so many laypeople have come to help in the ministry of the Church; bringing the faith to the people has *strengthened* the faith. When Dr. Nemeh runs into obstacles, he must remember that Jesus is the example he must follow. Jesus was not accepted by everyone He approached. What's sad is that there are people in the Church who don't have a feeling of acceptance for Dr. Nemeh due to either jealousy or their own lack of faith.

"However, and Issam would say the same thing, it's your faith that makes you well. God *can* work miracles. When Issam prays over people he is just an instrument God uses in doing His work. And that intimate time with each person, during the prayer, is like my one-on-one time with my Confirmation candidates. Those private moments can be powerful.

"There is more healing than is seen; there is more healing than is perceived. Healing doesn't save if there is no spiritual healing."

Part Three

VISIONS
OF
FAMILY

༈

23

An Arranged Marriage

It was a beautiful day in the last week of August 1982. Issam had gone along with his two roommates to the Ghazoul family home in West Park, Ohio. The houses on these quiet streets are mostly turn-of-the-century, built solid and spacious but not showy. The streets are lined with lots of trees under whose branches thousands of parochial school children in uniforms have trudged through the decades.

The Ghazoul home was located on a side street just off Rocky River Drive, the avenue otherwise known to native Clevelanders as "Holy Drive" because along a two-mile stretch are located St. Patrick's Church, Our Lady of Angels Church, the convent and chapel of the Poor Clare Colettine Nuns, and St. Joseph Academy. Tony and Kalima Ghazoul's children had attended Our Lady of Angels School, and later the two boys, Myron and Johnny, went to St. Ignatius High School, and the three girls, Kathy, Debbie, and Judy, entered St. Joseph Academy.

As the weather at the end of the summer rallied to impress the three young physicians who were seated on the Ghazoul family's enclosed front porch, twenty-six-year-old Kathy was entertaining them with stories of their homeland. She had just returned after spending a summer in Syria, the birthplace of both her parents as well as these three men. Kathy's mother served lunch and then disappeared inside, leaving the foursome to chat.

Kathy was animated as she regaled Dr. Taher Koussayer and Dr. Aboud Raslan with news from back home. They leaned in, soaking up all the details. Taher's mother, who was also Aboud's paternal aunt, had been a gracious hostess to Kathy during her stay in Homs, Syria, sending Kathy home with "care packages" in her suitcase for Taher and Aboud. They had come to fetch the bundles, but they stayed to hear news of their families. Kathy had only just been introduced to Dr. Issam Nemeh for the first time, so Issam did not insert himself very much into the conversation. From time to time Issam glanced at the pages of his red leather-bound Bible, but mostly he kept his eye on this dark-haired dynamo.

The next day Issam telephoned Kathy and asked her to a movie. She begged off because of jet lag. Two minutes later the Ghazoul telephone rang again. It was Aboud and he was outraged. He took umbrage that she had turned down his shy roommate. He defended Issam as the nicest man she could ever meet, scolded her for having embarrassed Issam with her refusal, and insisted that she apologize.

Why she relented she did not know, but she did. She called Issam and said, "You know, I guess I'm not too jet-lagged after all."

That night Issam took her to the Westgate Cinema in Westlake, Ohio, not far from Kathy's home, to see the box-office hit *E.T.* Kathy fell asleep during the movie. Afterward Issam took her to the restaurant of her choice. She chose the Ground

Round, a casual place best known for serving big bowls of pea-nuts at every table; guests tossed the empty shells onto the floor as they munched.

Issam called her the next day and asked if he could come over to see her. "Yes, of course," she was surprised to hear her-self answer. He came the following day as well, and it was on that third visit that he knew.

Here is a good girl, he thought. *I have found her.* He called Syria to tell his father he had met his life-mate. "I see beauty in her spirit. She impresses me so much. There is a kind of self-sacrifice in her: you ask her and she will do anything for you. She is always, always going extra miles for other people; there is so much care in her about others." There was also a spirit of endurance about her that appealed to Issam because he knew that stamina would be important in the years ahead. She had strength and faith like his father. She exuded the patience he admired in his paternal grandmother. Very precious to Issam was her quality of being able to forsake personal needs in the service of others. He saw all this in just three days.

Kathy could not explain "them" to herself or anyone else. She didn't have the heart *not* to spend time with Issam. He was unlike the lively men she had previously gravitated toward; he was so serious. In fact, by spending so much time with him she became estranged from her friends. They called, wonder-ing what she was up to. Was she dating someone? "No," she answered. "Not really." Yet she and Issam saw each other every day. Clearly something was drawing her to him.

He *was* interesting, and in time she came to understand that he was brilliant. Issam's mind was wide ranging and he could converse on any topic: science, politics, current affairs, culture, history, and the Bible. His facility with languages amazed her.

She was bilingual, but he could speak *seven* languages! He was curious, too, and he sweetly asked her questions no one else had ever thought to ask. What kind of prayer did she pray? Was it conversational? Who guided her spiritually?

She told him that she had always felt a strong connection to Blessed Mother. She wore a Blessed Mother medallion around her neck, carried her rosary everywhere, and, since childhood, had prayed the rosary every day. She told him that a terrible car accident had happened during her vacation in Syria, and that she believed Yahdra, the Arabic name for Blessed Mother, had saved her life.

"Oh," Issam murmured, both distressed that Kathy had been in harm's way and intrigued at Blessed Mother's intervention. "What happened?"

Kathy told him she had made a quick trip to town to buy ice for a picnic. At the time she was staying with her uncle and aunt in the Ghazoul ancestral hometown, Wadi el-Majawer, near Machta. Relatives had come from as far away as Saudi Arabia to meet up with their American cousin, and a fun picnic outing had been planned in the valley below the Mountain of the Blessed Mother, where they would spread blankets on the banks of the Miltakah River and just be together.

Picnics in Syria are not much different from picnics in America, Kathy learned, because just as everyone assembled at her uncle's home, someone shouted out that they needed ice. Bassam Shadah, who had just acquired a gorgeous new trophy car, immediately volunteered to run the errand to fetch ice from the nearby village. "Who wants to come with me?" called Bassam. In a split second Kathy, who always chose motion over stasis, answered, "I will!"

The route to town required driving along a skimpy ribbon of road called the Kooh el-Waday, which hugged tightly the Mountain of the Blessed Mother. Kathy and Bassam drove east down this road, bought ice, and then retraced their path, heading further west to meet up with the group. While she and Bassam chatted, Kathy looked out her open window, admiring the rocky face of the mountain named after the woman who was her spiritual guide.

Another road, the Kooh el-Kafroun, runs for several miles parallel to the two-lane road on which Bassam and Kathy were traveling, and along the way it curves in a severe right hook, like an umbrella handle, so as to ease its traffic onto the road going into Machta. Neither the R-shaped curve nor the Kooh el-Waday leaves room for error. The rocky face of the mountain is on one side, and on the other is a sheer precipice that offers a gasping plummet down a rocky abyss with a final resting place on the riverbank below.

As Bassam approached the point where the hook conjoined the road upon which he and Kathy were traveling, his Mercedes encountered a pickup truck gone wild. The curve of the road proved too extreme for the truck's speed. The pickup sideswiped the Mercedes, muscling it into the rocky mountainside, and then zoomed onward, never pausing in its destructive course. Bassam's car smashed into the mountain, then skittered across the roadway, rolling twice, as if it were a black die thrown from the hand of a giant. On the third roll Kathy shouted to Blessed Mother. *"Yahdra! Yahdra!"* The car ceased its wild tumble and froze.

Kathy could see nothing but blue sky. She listened for Bassam but heard only a creepy, insidious sound, like the creak of a wooden ship at its mooring.

"Bassam. If you are alive and you can hear me, I want you

to know that I'm going to count to three. On the count of three *I'm* going to crawl out *my* window and *you're* going to crawl out *your* window."

Silence.

"*Wahid.* One. *Ithnan.* Two. *Thalatha.* Three."

As Kathy scrambled out the open window the Blessed Mother medallion she wore around her neck clinked against the car. Just as her feet hit terra firma she caught a glimpse of Bassam lowering himself over the driver's door.

It was a good thing they coordinated their escape. No sooner had they achieved their footing than they heard the awful sound of a slow-motion disintegration of wood. The front end of the Mercedes had been balancing on a tree branch no bigger than Kathy's forearm, like a vulture perched on a toothpick.

The doomed sedan hesitated, as though it dreaded what would happen next. It tipped away from the mountain and then paused. With one last groan it gave up the struggle, relinquished its ridiculous balancing act, and fell, nose first, bouncing and crashing down the mountainside. The remains of Bassam's car came to rest on the banks of the Miltakah River not far from a patchwork of brightly colored blankets spread gaily on the grass where thirty-eight picnickers awaited the arrival of ice.

Issam and Kathy continued seeing each other throughout the fall of 1982. Each time Issam came calling at the Ghazoul home he was dressed with impeccable taste. Kathy grew to understand Issam's instinctive affinity for fine things, but she noticed also that he did not indulge himself; he just recognized and appreciated quality. He was polite and her parents loved him. And he was generous in every way. Generosity was very important to Kathy because her parents had lived and had raised their family by this credo: *Give and God will give you back. God always gives you back.*

She did not tell Issam the story of the other close call she had experienced during her vacation in Syria. If it were not for this quality of generosity that was so highly prized by everyone in the Ghazoul family, she might very well have been engaged to marry another man. As she grew more and more enchanted by Issam, she thought about how Blessed Mother always seemed to be guiding and protecting her in every way, because this other Syrian doctor who was interested in her would have been the wrong match for her.

It was mid-August, and she was still at her uncle and aunt's home in Wadi el-Majawer. Kathy noticed a big hullabaloo going on in the kitchen. Her aunt was overseeing the preparation of a huge luncheon celebration for forty guests. When Kathy offered to help with the cooking, her apron-clad aunts just giggled and shooed her away.

Kathy did not know that Salim, a young Syrian physician she had met in July, was coming, along with his family, with the intention of making a formal, public proposal of marriage, as was the custom in Syria. Kathy's aunt and uncle were pulling out all the stops for this important event.

Kathy had met Salim when she traveled from Damascus to the northern city of Aleppo, one of the oldest continuously inhabited cities in the world. It is said that Abraham, the patriarch of Jews, Christians, and Muslims, camped in Aleppo. Strategically positioned where many important commercial trade roads converge, Aleppo has enjoyed prosperity and status since prebiblical days. While visiting the city, Kathy took in the major tourist attractions: the Great Mosque, the

Khan al-Gumruk, the Byzantine cathedral, Madrasa al-Firdaus (the "Madrasa of Paradise"), the Achiqbash House. But the visit was, for her, more about connecting with cousins enrolled at the local University of Aleppo. Cousin Nadeem showed her around the off-campus house he shared with friends, one of whom was Salim, who became quite smitten with the vivacious American.

One evening Kathy and Salim were walking on the streets of Issah, a shopping district where the sidewalks are cordoned off in the evenings and young people stroll beneath twinkling lights in a carnival-like atmosphere. The two paused at a vendor's cart. The vendor and his young son were selling what was, for Kathy, a reminder of home: itty-bitty boxes of Chiclets. Kathy felt a pang of homesickness. She decided to buy some. Reaching into her purse, she drew out coins and offered them to the vendor in an upturned palm. In Arabic she asked, "How much do you want for the gum?"

Salim reacted swiftly. He grabbed her outstretched hand. "No," he reprimanded. "You don't do it that way. Find out what he charges first, then get your money out."

"Are you *kidding* me?" Kathy asked, and looked up into his face. She could see that he was not kidding, and she was horrified. "This man is trying to make a *living*," she said. "His *little boy* is *working* right alongside him."

She couldn't believe Salim was cold to the situation. Where was his compassion? She decided that if Salim didn't get it, she couldn't explain it to him. "I'll pay for gum the way I want to."

That was all she needed to see of Salim's character. Generosity was one of the most highly prized attributes on Planet Ghazoul; an ungenerous nature was something Kathy could not abide. Salim didn't pick up on the judgment she had made based on the Chiclets incident. He never seemed to realize that his behavior had given Kathy a window into his spirit.

So when Salim arrived and presented flowers and candy to the hostess, and introduced his parents and brother, Kathy's only thought was, *Uh-oh.* She dreaded a marriage proposal because she would have to refuse Salim in front of everyone, and this embarrassment would reflect back on his entire family.

In the Syrian custom of *mezza,* a table was laden with hors d'oeuvres and drinks. Kathy's uncle winked at her and she felt sick inside. Guests were mingling on the veranda and throughout the opened-up rooms in the sprawling home until Kathy's aunt called everyone to lunch.

There was homemade hummus, chicken and lamb kabobs, tabbouleh, stuffed grape leaves, eggplant dishes, and kibbeh— ground lamb presented with vegetables and rice. There were *sfeha*—meat-and-spinach pies. A tasty *qubba*—meat, pinenuts, and spices rolled in a crust of cracked wheat bulgur. *Mun saf,* a dish combining almonds, pine nuts, and meat resting on a bed of rice, commanded center stage. It was a table at which royalty could dine.

Kathy's uncle, *Ammo* Deeb, began the meal with a toast. Cousin Emad followed, offering a toast to the host and hostess. Then Salim rose from his chair. Kathy's heart sank. She looked up at this handsome, nice, educated young man and felt so, so sorry for him.

At six foot three Salim towered over the seated guests. He waited until bits of table conversation fluttered softly into silence and all eyes were on him. He raised his double whiskey on the rocks and had gotten two words out when there was an explosion: the glass in his hand shattered.

Crystal shards sprayed upward like bullets, piercing the

prisms of the chandelier and causing *them* to splinter. Crystal rained down on the guests. Crystal confetti lay twinkling in their hair. Syrupy whiskey splashed their faces and arms. The lavish platters were poisoned.

A hideous silence followed the explosion. Salim's face went white. His parents stared, horrified. What everyone instantly understood was that this disaster was a sign—a very bad sign, and as such it could not be clearer: this union was not meant to be.

A very odd coda to the afternoon was yet to be played out. Kathy's uncle, aunt, and cousins retired to their bedrooms for the four o'clock siesta. Everyone was exhausted from the enormous effort of cooking, washing dishes, and cleaning debris, as well as the emotions of the day. Dullness sulked in the thick afternoon as they sighed in their beds. Heat throbbed in the droning stillness. Kathy could not sleep, so she wandered the seven-bedroom ranch, restless. She replayed the events of the day in her mind. She alternated between pity for Salim and feelings of empowerment, because she knew she was meant for other things. She paced and prayed while the family napped.

Inside the quiet house the telephone jangled. Anxious to spare the household from being awakened, Kathy rushed to pick up the receiver.

"*Ahlan?* Hello?"

"I met the man you're going to marry."

Given the upsetting luncheon debacle Kathy had just experienced, this was an especially jarring way to be greeted by her mother, who was calling from the States.

———

During the months that Kathy was summering in Syria, Taher and Aboud were in Cleveland attending classes to improve their English. There they met another Syrian doctor who had just moved to the area. They liked him. He was quiet, intelligent, serious about his studies, gentlemanly, and witty. Would he maybe like to room with them? Indeed, he would. Taher and Aboud were tenants in one of her father's apartment rental suites, but they found a bigger apartment and the duo became a trio.

Taher and Aboud had been befriended by their landlord many times and had come to feel as though the Ghazoul residence was their home away from home. They looked forward to introducing their new friend to the warm hospitality typically extended by the Ghazoul family. In mid-August they brought Issam with them when they stopped by for a visit, and Kalima somehow knew with certainty that this was the right man for Kathy.

After they left, Kalima, never before a meddler in her children's affairs and certainly not a proponent of arranged marriages, placed a transatlantic phone call to tell her daughter about this remarkable young man. She was not surprised when, after announcing she had met the man Kathy would marry, her fiercely independent daughter retorted, "Mom! I'm not going to marry *any*one! I've got things I want to do!"

"Kathy," her mother repeated, slowly and in an all-knowing tone. "I met the man you're going to marry."

"If you like him so much, *you* marry him!"

One month after that phone call Kathy was spending every day with Issam. It seemed to Kathy that Blessed Mother had delivered this man straight to her doorstep. The contrast between Issam and her would-be suitor in Syria was so marked that Kathy could clearly see how right Issam was for her. And even though just weeks earlier Kathy had been so sure she would pursue a career in either politics or law, those personal plans had been put aside by this generous, spiritual, sensitive man who had captivated her heart.

On Christmas Eve Issam drove to the Ghazoul home in his baby blue Mustang II. He helped Kathy into the car, waiting for her to arrange the folds of her coat until he shut the door. He drove to Westgate Mall, where they had gone to the cinema on their first date, pulled into a parking space, and put the car in park. He turned to Kathy, pulled a ring from his pocket, and offered it to her, watching her face as he did so.

"Oh," she said softly, looking at the beautiful diamond solitaire with two side stones. "This is very pretty! Thank you." She slipped it on her finger.

Then they drove to St. Maron's Church on Carnegie Avenue near East Ninth Street in downtown Cleveland, where Kathy had been baptized, to share midnight Mass with the family.

For Issam, there was no falling in love with Kathy. Issam believes love is a decision. When one makes the decision to love, he says, it is a decision for life. Once he had made his decision about Kathy, loving her was effortless and eternal. For Kathy, too, there was no falling in love with Issam. There was just the soulfulness of *loving*.

They set their wedding date: Saturday, April 9, 1983, the day before Issam's twenty-ninth birthday, only seven months after they had met. They would be married at St. Maron's Church, a Syrian and Lebanese parish named for a Syrian missionary who, sometime around 400 A.D., initiated the conversion of people from paganism to Christianity in Syria, the sparks of which touched off the spread of Christianity to Lebanon. The saint was monastic, ascetic, and lived in the style of a Thoreauvian naturalist. He was also a notable healer, curing physical disease, sickness, and ailments of all kinds in the course of his evangelical career. He saw in healing a spiritual opportunity, for he viewed wounded, confused, questioning souls as containing unmined riches, and he prayed over pagans and Christians alike.

During their engagement Kathy came to appreciate that Issam was unlike any man she had ever known. His whole approach to life was different. He maintained an unswerving focus on the important aspects of life, like compassion and service to others. He would ruminate about lofty ideals and spiritual truths and then reveal his concerns and deeply held convictions in philosophical discussions she found enthralling. He told her, "I want to share with you. I want to tell you everything. I'm here on this earth on a mandate; God sent me here for a mission. God has gifted me, and little by little you will come to understand what He wants from me." Issam had known since childhood that his destiny was to fulfill a significant role in the world. His mission was very clear-cut but he spoke in mysterious phrases. He told her, "You stay strong; you stand with me. You have to be my partner in this." Kathy was having trouble grasping much of what he was saying, but she found a helper who tutored her in the art of understanding her fiancé: Issam's father, Wadi Nemeh.

Kathy quickly grew to love *Ammo* Wadi. He would call from Syria and she would spend hours talking to him, curled up on the couch in the basement, where no one would think to look for her. *Ammo* Wadi's telephone calls became this bride-to-be's bedtime stories.

Ammo Wadi told her that he had been orphaned and then raised by his grandparents. He grew up in an era of tremendous discrimination against Christians in Syria; Christians were being killed continually throughout the 1920s and 1930s. Those who survived did so by running away into the mountains and by their faith.

He described Issam's mother, Nadia Jabbour Nemeh, as a classic beauty who was known for her gourmet cooking. He said Issam's siblings—Marwan, sister Fadia, and younger brother, Hassan—were very close when they were young. They had grown into quite an accomplished bunch. All three of the boys had become medical doctors and Fadia was a pharmacist. But *Ammo* Wadi admitted there had been something unique about Issam from the beginning. "They are all bright," he said of his children, "but he is different. Although he has always been wise beyond his years, he is special because of his gift of sensitivity."

He told Kathy of the baby who never cried and enchanted her with stories of Issam as a young boy. He said Issam grew into a wiry, athletic boy known for his climbing dexterity. He would scale a tree and scramble over the porch roof and into the second-floor windows rather than walk through the front door; he was all about challenging himself. He would often disappear from home, and when the family discovered that he was missing they always knew they could find him at St. Vincent's Church.

Ammo Wadi told Kathy about Issam's years abroad. He told her about the weekly letters Issam had written home while he was in medical school, letters so precious to Wadi he has saved every one of them. With awe in his voice he told her, "The letters are so deep, they should be published!" And Kathy learned from *Ammo* Wadi that, against all odds, Issam had been awarded a visa to the United States. This happened at the very same time a fun-loving, Bambi-eyed beauty from West Park, Ohio, traveled to Damascus and began a summer in Syria.

In June of 1982, Kathy arrived in Damascus and was greeted by her first host and hostess, General Elias Mourany and his wife, Leila—Kalima's cousin—and their daughter, Sahar. Kathy stayed with the Mouranys for two weeks. She was treated to a new adventure each day. The first morning the general told his wife, daughter, and houseguest as he went off to work, "Be ready!" He came breezing in the door earlier than usual that afternoon and took them to the Umayyad Mosque and the Citadel, two of the most revered holy sites in Damascus. Then he treated them to dinner in a wonderful restaurant. Such outings became their routine. One day they saw the gorgeous ruins of Seidnaya. Another, they went to Maʿlula, where Aramaic is spoken. Kathy walked the courtyard of the Azem Palace and roamed the National Museum. They visited Bosra and saw the remains of one of the largest theaters ever constructed in Roman times.

Kathy strolled down one particular street many times on her way to the shopping district. Along the way she noticed a silver-haired gentleman who sat in a rocking chair on the wide front porch of his house, surveying the street scene. He was fair skinned and had a kindly face. She always smiled at him and he returned her smiles. He reminded her of Academy Award–winning actor and comedian Red Buttons, and his gentle eyes stayed in her memory.

One week before her wedding, Issam's parents flew to Cleveland and Kathy and Issam were there to greet them at the airport. Kathy recognized her father-in-law at once. She knew him by the sweet, Red Buttons smile and by his kindly eyes that crinkled at the corners.

It was then that Kathy realized Blessed Mother had been connecting the dots, drawing a line from one front porch in Damascus, Syria, to another front porch in West Park, Ohio, and by doing so had outlined a marriage arranged by God.

24.

Family Ties

As a young woman Kathy suffered severe pelvic pain from endometriosis and had been warned by her obstetrician-gynecologist, Dr. Hew, that she might not be able to have children. But Issam prayed over Kathy and told her to have faith she would be healed. She never again experienced the horrible pelvic pain that had plagued her for years.

In June 1983, just weeks after Issam and Kathy's wedding, the Ghazoul extended family attended the wedding reception of a relative. As the band played and people danced, Kathy's father, normally gregarious and the life of the party, sat alone at a table, pale and sweating.

Issam pulled Kathy aside. "Go to the bar and get a glass of whiskey."

Kathy was confused. Issam never touched the stuff. "You want a glass of *whiskey*?" Issam shook his head. "You want *me* to have a glass of whiskey?" she asked. This was an even more ridiculous notion.

"Your father is having a heart attack. The whiskey is to open the blood vessels."

Kathy hustled to the bar.

Returning with the whiskey, Kathy beheld a striking tableau: Issam and her father standing beside each other, utterly
still, in bizarre contrast to the music and dancing of the wedding celebration. Issam's eyes were closed and his head was
bowed. His left hand rested on Tony's upper back. His right
hand covered the left side of Tony's chest. Kathy felt as if she
was watching through a keyhole, so alone did Issam and Tony
appear to be. She hesitated to penetrate the aura that seemed to
encircle the two men. But there was the matter of the whiskey.

"Issam."

Issam took a deep breath, opened his eyes very slowly, and
nodded to acknowledge Kathy. Taking the glass from her hand,
he said, "*Ammo*, I want you to drink this." Tony did as he was
told.

Issam, Kathy, and the rest of the family sped Tony to Huron Road Hospital. That night Dr. Michael Hanna performed
an emergency catheterization, and Dr. Elias Husni did open-
heart surgery, during which he discovered four blockages. He
later told the family, "He should have died."

Kathy pulled Issam aside. "How do you explain this? How
did he live?"

Issam pointed up. "That was God's will."

But that little tableau.

Kathy turned that memory over in her mind again and
again, as if it were a snow globe, and each time she lingered
in fascination at the images fluttering across her mind's eye.
Issam, standing so cool, so composed in the midst of all that
activity. It was his stillness that was so odd.

That vignette was Kathy's first hint of what Issam was all
about.

———

She became pregnant five months after their wedding. Although Issam was excited to meet his first child, on the day that Kathy was admitted to the hospital with a high fever, Issam had to be in Boston, Massachusetts, to take a required medical exam. When fetal monitors began to register that the baby was in distress, Dr. Hew performed an emergency Cesarean section, and delivered a beautiful baby girl at eight-thirty in the evening on June 12, 1984. Kathy and Issam would name her Fadia Marie, after Issam's sister and Blessed Mother.

The Ghazoul family joined Kathy and the baby in the recovery room while Dr. Hew called Issam and filled him in on the medical details of his wife's C-section. Then Dr. Hew passed the phone to Kathy. She described the baby to her husband. "She looks like a Nemeh, Issam. She's all Nemeh."

He murmured, "I hope she has your eyes."

Myron Ghazoul collected Issam from the airport the next evening and brought him straightaway to the hospital. Walking into Kathy's room, Issam felt momentarily confused. His senses were overloaded by the sight that greeted him. He thought that maybe he was in the wrong place, because the room resembled a baby store. Flowers, baby clothes, and plush animals were everywhere. Issam tried to shake the vision of the pink landscape so that he might locate his wife in her bed. Then he smiled. He walked a few steps nearer and there beside Kathy's bed was the bassinet.

He bent over. He drank in this lovely sight, overwhelmed with the beauty of his newborn daughter. He knew in that first moment that God had sent her to *him*. His eyes filled with tears. He heard Kathy ask in a small voice, "Did I do a good job?"

Tears spilled over and streamed down his cheeks by way of an answer. Then he picked up this little miracle. He lifted her to his face and he baptized her in his love with his tears.

And then he began covering her with millions of kisses.

I ssam's parents arranged for the new family to travel to Damascus for the baby's baptism. While the new family was there they traveled with Issam's mother to Latakia to visit Issam's grandmother and his uncle, Michael Jabbour.

Latakia, a gorgeous, ancient seaport city on the coast of the Mediterranean about 220 miles north of Damascus, is renowned for its pristine shoreline sandwiched between brilliant blue waters and green mountains thickly wooded with pine and oak trees. Archaeological evidence supports that the city has been continuously inhabited since a thousand years before the Christian era. As a boy Issam had spent his summers swimming every day in Latakia's sparkling waters, as his parents owned a second home there. The beauty was breathtaking, but the deeper attraction for young Issam was his uncle.

Uncle Michael's brilliant mind had always fascinated Issam, yet Issam was troubled that his uncle was too scientific to allow for spirituality. The two would talk for hours, Issam explaining his theory that there is no separation between God and science, and telling his uncle why he saw religion and medicine existing on one continuum. Issam had the great satisfaction of knowing that he had played a role in opening his uncle's mind to a greater awareness of spirituality.

Uncle Michael had been in medical school in Austria when he was involved in a horrendous car accident that left him blind. "His professor of neurosurgery brought him home," Issam told

Kathy. "The neurosurgeon sat in my grandmother's house sobbing. My father was there, and he asked, 'Why are you crying, Professor?' 'Because Austria *and the world* lost a mind that will not repeat itself,' the professor answered. 'It is a great, great loss for this country.'"

After a pleasant drive from Damascus, Issam, Kathy, baby Fadia, and Issam's mother, Nadia, arrived at the home Uncle Michael shared with his mother. Issam's grandmother answered the door and clutched her heart, she was so moved to see her grandson. She hugged his wife and kissed his baby, wrapped her arms around her daughter, Nadia, then led them into her living room. From a room tucked away in another part of the house, Kathy heard a man's voice saying, "*Ruh*. His soul. *Habib albi*. I feel his soul in the room. I feel his very being in the room! I can smell his soul." And then he was standing there with his head tilted up, his arms outstretched to the soul he recognized. He was crying. "Issam," he choked out between sobs. He exclaimed in Arabic, German, and finally in English, "My love, my life!" Issam and Michael embraced. The immense love this man felt for Issam took Kathy's breath away.

When it came time for Michael to meet Kathy, he did what he did with everyone in his life: he smelled her. His mother began to apologize but Kathy reassured her it was fine. Then with his hands he felt her from the crown of her hair down to her forehead. He felt the feathery eyelashes fanning her almond-shaped eyes. His fingers slid down her high cheekbones and traced her full mouth.

"Ahhh," he breathed. "Issam, *hiya jamila*. She's beautiful!" he pronounced appreciatively.

Issam grinned. Then he placed Fadia in Michael's arms. Michael was enthralled. He smelled this new soul, examined her with his hands, and settled on the couch holding her in the crook of his arm. She fussed a little, he crooned a lullaby, and she fell asleep. She napped the entire afternoon in his arms.

Issam had brought Michael gifts: a robe, some shirts, cologne. After a while they went to church. Issam took Kathy aside and asked if she would mind if he slept at his grandmother's house during the four nights they planned to be in Latakia. She and the baby would stay in his parents' chalet with Nadia. "I just need to spend time with my uncle," he said.

"Of course, Issam. I will be fine. Enjoy your time with him."

At the end of the visit saying good-bye was wrenching. Michael held Issam as though he were trying to memorize the feel of him. He gave Kathy a message as a farewell gift: "I need to tell you how special, how gifted, and how close to Christ he is. You need to stand by him because he's going to be very misunderstood. You cannot walk away when that happens. You are his partner. You were chosen for him."

Kathy didn't appreciate what he meant at the time. Later she understood these words to be prophetic. She loved seeing Issam through Uncle Michael's blindness, insight that reflected the essence, spirit, soul, and distinctive goodness of her husband.

25.

❧

The Mandate

The Nemehs' second child was born on March 18, 1988, and this time Issam was standing beside Kathy during the Cesarean delivery of the child four-year-old big sister Fadia would name Ashley Marie. Although Issam was immersed in his residency at Meridia Huron Road Hospital, he was able to take a month off in the fall to travel to Syria with Kathy, Fadia, and six-month-old Ashley to attend his sister Fadia's wedding in Damascus.

After the wedding weekend the Nemehs went to Kafroun, a little town where Kathy's first cousin Layla Saada lived with her husband, Hanna. Layla had prepared the master bedroom for her guests by pushing two big beds together and placing pillows all around. Fadia and Ashley fell asleep in this soft nest.

Meanwhile cousins and friends came by the house. A fire was lit against the mid-October chill, and the family sat around swapping stories and sipping tea. At one point in the evening, Issam slipped away to check on the girls. Going back to the fireside, he turned a corner and as he did so an apparition of Mary the Mother of Sorrows appeared to him. Issam felt her purity intensely. A veil covered her hair. Her eyes were dark. Her face displayed no expression or emotion. He knew from this brief event that something significant was going to happen.

It was nearly three in the morning by the time the last guest left. The weary travelers said good-night to their hosts and closed the beautiful frosted-glass bedroom door behind them. Kathy climbed into her side of the bed beside Ashley; Issam lay down on the other side next to Fadia. Kathy fell asleep facing outward, toward the windowed wall. Issam drifted into a light slumber.

Issam and Kathy were awakened by a sudden strong wind that shook the window shutters. Issam opened his eyes to a soft blue light shining on the other side of the bedroom door. Floating, the blue light moved through the translucent glass. It settled at the foot of the bed. It was she. She wore robes of robin's egg blue and dark navy. Light emanated from her, radiance that was both *of* her and *was* her.

The Mother of Sorrows began by telling Fadia to remain prayerful. She told the child, "You must be very sweet." Unafraid, Fadia talked with her. Then, turning her attention to Ashley, Blessed Mother began singing. Tears came to Issam's eyes, her voice was so angelic. When his six-month-old daughter began singing back to her, he knew immediately what was happening: Ashley was receiving a gift. Too frightened to look, Kathy listened as they sang softly to each other, like student and teacher. Issam watched the whole thing.

Issam sensed that Blessed Mother had a message for him, so he got out of bed, went to the chair in the room, sat down, and waited. Soon he perceived a subtle shift in the ambience of the room, and the Mother of Sorrows appeared before him.

In his vision, she reached into a pouch made of fine leather that had suddenly appeared slung across the back of the chair in which he was sitting. She pulled out a piece of pale yellow fruit, shaped like a lemon. By earthly standards, the fruit was enormous, more like an oversized pomegranate than a lemon. *Fruit from paradise*, thought Issam.

He watched as the huge piece of fruit floated from Blessed Mother's hands toward him, where it paused, levitating. Then invisible hands seemed to peel the fruit to expose its inner sections. Each section was precisely equal in size and shape. These sections separated from one another and scattered.

Issam asked Blessed Mother what she was trying to show him. She explained that these equal pieces were symbolic of the children of all the churches, and that she wanted him to gather them up and place them back into the leather pouch. Issam understood. So he started grabbing the fruit sections from where they hovered in the air. He placed them back into the leather pocket, then turned to her, a question in his eyes as to what was expected of him next.

She answered by showing him a vision of a pale blue church sitting on top of a hill. It was a heavenly looking church. He could tell it had been built specially. She showed him every detail of its construction. Blessed Mother told him he would be instrumental in doing something for all Christians, and that he would help her build this church of equality.

He doubted his worthiness for such a task, and Blessed Mother became very disappointed in him. Issam hastened to explain, "Oh, no—please forgive me. I do not doubt you! I doubt myself! I don't see myself as fitting this purpose. Even if I start doing this now, I'm going to be rejected." In her eyes Issam saw a softening, and she told him this would be his job for many years to come.

———————

D r. Nemeh perceived the encounter with the Mother of Sorrows as a mandate to help gather disparate religions and diverse worshippers into what Blessed Mother called the Church of All. It explains his overarching philosophy of acceptance, nonjudgment, and love. In the next few years the doctor would continue to build his medical practice so that he would have a platform upon which he could minister to the thousands of souls God had told him would come to him for prayer. And he would become father to two more children. One would rescue him, and the other would prove the strength of his faith.

⁓

26

Holding On, Letting Go

On March 10, 1990, Issam and Kathy were blessed with the birth of a third daughter. Whereas baby Fadia had cried a great deal because of lactose intolerance, and, from birth, Ashley was always up to some dramatic hilarity, Debbie was different. She was quiet, peaceful, and nondemanding, just as her father had been when he was a baby.

When Wadi and Nadia came from Syria to meet their new grandchild and Wadi got his first look at her, he exclaimed, "My mom! I see my mom in her!" Thus was born something very special between *Giddo*—"Grandfather" in Arabic—and this little girl, because the miracle of her genetics connected him to his past. Each time he saw this grandchild he greeted her by saying, "You are the love of your grandfather's heart." Then he would turn and explain, as if everyone didn't already know, "That's my mother there in her face."

As time went on, it became apparent that God was up to something specific with Debbie: God used her to reel Issam back into the family circle. In the early to mid-1990s, Issam's anesthesiology practice was keeping him at work almost constantly. Since the apparition of Blessed Mother in Syria, Issam had redoubled his efforts to accomplish his missions. The family had learned to carry on without him, but Debbie yearned for her daddy. He was the light of her life.

When she was old enough to walk, Debbie was known for fetching Issam's pillow and smuggling it into her bed, where she would bury her nose in it and wait for him to come home. Every evening she would stand like a sentry, camouflaged by the huge indoor tree Kathy set in the front picture window, watching out the window for Issam's car. When she caught sight of him pulling in the drive she raced to greet him.

He taught her how to ride a bike. As a weekend ritual he would paint her nails. She loved it when he painted her toenails red, all the while laughing because he felt so silly. She laughed because he was laughing. Soon she couldn't remember who had started the whole thing, but it didn't matter anyway because their laughter blended into one big feeling of happiness.

And she amazed him. Issam told Kathy, wonder in his voice, "She's like an *angel*."

In 1994 the family made plans to attend Myron's wedding in Syria. Issam went to the airport to help Kathy and the kids board the plane, then turned to leave after kissing them good-bye. He had planned to stay home for another couple of weeks before flying to Syria, but four-year-old Debbie did not know that. Debbie watched her father walk down the aisle and off the plane and an expression of horror came over her face. *"What?"* she cried. "Do you mean Daddy is not going *with* us?"

She was traumatized. Wadi telephoned his son after the family had been in Syria for a week, telling him, "Issam, you must close up your office and come here."

"I cannot do that," Issam responded, surprised. *What on earth was his father talking about?* he wondered.

"Your little one is pining for you. She will not eat. She cannot sleep. She is making herself sick. You have to come here as soon as possible."

It was true. Debbie was inconsolable. Issam canceled his office appointments and flew to Syria.

Kathy focused on cultivating a home that was a haven for Issam. She had fun with the girls, and Issam was thrilled with his daughters. Still, she longed for a son. She wanted Issam's parents, who had been blessed with six granddaughters, to have at least one grandchild who would carry on the family name. While she wrestled with this unfulfilled dream, her uncle Eddie Maroon was struggling with terminal cancer.

Eddie Maroon is Kathy's mother's first cousin. From their wedding day forward, Uncle Eddie was in awe of Issam. He could see that there was something uniquely spiritual in him. Their paths often crossed at Fairview Hospital because Eddie was the director of pharmacy and Issam was a resident surgeon. Issam would sometimes stop in at the pharmacy to talk with Eddie.

Dolores, Eddie's wife, also thought the world of Issam. She came to understand that he had a very special calling. An incident with her grandmother, *Sitto* Lumya, solidified this belief. *Sitto* Lumya suffered a bad fall, and the family brought her to Fairview Hospital emergency room. The doctors and nurses were having difficulty communicating with her because she spoke Arabic, so Issam was called to the emergency room to bridge the language gulf. After *Sitto* Lumya was admitted to the hospital, Issam stopped in each night after rounds. They talked. They prayed. *Sitto* Lumya recovered. The Maroon family was forever grateful for the special attention Issam had given their matriarch.

Then Dolores's world unraveled in June 1991 when Eddie was diagnosed with non-Hodgkin's lymphoma. Normally, this type of cancer is treatable, but in Eddie's case the cancer had metastasized. The months between the diagnosis and the holiday season were filled with shocking adjustments to the exigencies of Eddie's illness.

Finally, just before Thanksgiving, Eddie was admitted to the intensive care unit at the Cleveland Clinic. The cancer had crept into the meninges and the cerebrospinal fluid. A shunt was inserted into his brain. His vital signs were collapsing. His pulse weakened until there was almost no pulse at all. Dolores and Eddie were holding hands when he invoked her maiden name, his pet name for her, and whispered, "I think we're losing it, Jalaytie." Dolores panicked. "No we're not!" she said. "You're going to get well. I'm not leaving you and we're going home together!" Remembering what Issam had done to help *Sitto* Lumya, Dolores called Kathy and asked if Issam would please come to the clinic where Eddie was dying and pray with him.

Issam went to the hospital and prayed beside Eddie. As he prayed, the vital signs on the monitor climbed almost as though they were elevator floor indicators. Issam did not leave the room until Eddie was fully revived, until Eddie had progressed from being a man on his deathbed with a barely measurable pulse to a patient with completely normal vital signs. To Issam, Eddie's recovery was another example of how religion and medicine exist on one continuum: what medicine is unable to accomplish is sometimes completed with the addition of a missing ingredient—prayer. Issam walked out of Eddie's hospital room confident that God had rearranged Eddie's physical systems on a molecular level. As he sat talking over coffee with Dolores in the cafeteria she told Issam about Eddie's wish to be home for Christmas. He reassured her, "Eddie will be home for Christmas. I can guarantee you that."

On December 23, 1991, Dolores left the hospital for the first time since Eddie had been admitted in November. She drove home as though she were being chased. She ran upstairs to the attic and lugged the Christmas tree from storage and then set it up in the front room. She flung some lights on the branches, skipping the ornaments entirely. Then she rushed back to the clinic. On Christmas Eve day, Eddie came home by ambulance, and when they wheeled him into the house the tree was lit.

Dolores turned the family room into a hospital-like environment. Issam, determined that Eddie should enjoy as much as possible in those last weeks of his life, came by every day to care for him.

One day in February while keeping watch over Eddie, Issam was grieving deeply. A little cloud of rainbow-colored sprinkles twinkling just outside the window caught his attention. These brightly colored flecks of light assembled and then swooped in through the window, making a whoosh sound as they curved into the room. In the space between two heartbeats the glinting crystals had re-formed into a tall, impressive figure standing beside Eddie's bed. It was an angel, transparent as crystal jewelry. The angel's iridescence sparkled with the colors of the aurora borealis and his eyes were golden, huge, and impenetrable. They gazed unblinkingly straight through Issam.

The whoosh roused Eddie from his nap, and he turned toward the sound. He, too, could see the messenger angel.

The angel commanded Issam, "Let him be. You are holding him back with your grief. You must not grieve over him anymore." The angel let this message resonate before adding, "It is time for him to come home."

Eddie looked at Issam with sad eyes and nodded ever so slightly.

"He's right," said Eddie. "It is time for me to go."

At that moment Dolores appeared in the archway between the kitchen and the family room. She felt an ominous presence. A knot tightened in her throat. She searched Eddie's and Issam's faces and her heart plummeted. Their expressions betrayed the presence she felt but could not see.

"What's going on?"

Neither man answered.

"What's going on?" she demanded, her tone turning on the jagged edge of fear. "There is something *here*. I can *feel* it!"

Issam soothed her, saying, "No, no, it is nothing."

She didn't believe him. Terror blazed in her eyes.

"We saw nothing, Dolores. It was nothing."

There was a trickle of tears coming from Eddie's eyes. He glanced at Issam. It was their secret. There would be plenty of time to tell her who had been there with them. For now, there was no need to frighten her any further.

Eddie died four days later.

27.

❧

Test of Faith

Kathy became pregnant a few months after her uncle passed away. Even before the pregnancy was confirmed she had a dream in which Uncle Eddie approached, a blanketed infant cradled in his arms. He handed her the bundle, saying, "This is my gift to you." When she peeked inside the blanket she saw a beautiful baby boy.

Dr. Steven Mazzone, Kathy's cousin and a radiologist at Fairview Hospital, performed all three of Kathy's ultrasounds. In the first, it was too early to tell whether the child was a boy or a girl. At the second ultrasound Steven was crowing, "I was really, really rooting for you, Kathy. It's a *boy!*"

He continued scanning. While she was still basking in the wonderful news, it occurred to Kathy that Steven had gotten very quiet. She studied him. He was acting nervous.

"What? You still think it's a boy, don't you?" she asked.

"Yes, yes, I swear it's a boy. Look—a boy." Steven printed a photo and handed it to her.

Issam and Kathy attended a cousin's wedding that weekend. The whole family was there, including Dr. Mazzone. At one point during the reception Kathy realized that she was alone at their table. Issam was gone. Johnny, Judy, Debbie, Myron—even Steven—everyone was missing. She spotted them huddled together. She knew in an instant that they were talking about her and her baby. She marched right up to the group and demanded, "I want to know what's going on."

"Nothing's going on. Everything's fine."

"Either tell me now or I'm going to cause a scene."

Dr. Mazzone shot a look around the group and relented. "There's something not quite right in the brain. I'm not sure you're going to be able to keep the baby. There's something attached at the forehead; the baby is very likely to be deformed and blind."

Kathy's mind whirled. They had just called her father-in-law in Syria and told him he had a grandson on the way.

She said, "Wait a minute, you're giving up already? Don't you believe in miracles?"

"Yes, but Kathy, it doesn't look good."

Issam, in his own quiet way, said just two words. *"Allah karim."* God is generous.

On the way home, Kathy asked her husband, "What do we do now?"

"We're going to go by faith. Whatever it is, it is." Then Issam reminded her of her dream about Uncle Eddie and finished by asking, "How can you doubt?"

Dr. Hew urged Kathy to undergo an amniocentesis but Issam objected. "I don't care what the baby is, we're going by faith." Kathy agreed. Issam prayed over Kathy and told her not to worry.

At the scheduled third ultrasound, Kathy held her rosary and beseeched Blessed Mother, *Go ahead and do your thing here . . . make this baby healthy,* she prayed.

Steven studied the fetal images. Finally, he said, "I can't explain this, but whatever was there is gone now. Everything is fine."

The baby's due date was April 24, but a healthy boy was delivered—no surprise here—by emergency C-section on March 29, 1993. Kathy cradled her baby and felt a new affinity with Blessed Mother. Kathy, too, was now the mother of a son. She named the dark-haired child after Issam's father, the storyteller who had shared tales of Issam's childhood with her before she was married many years ago. When choosing a middle name, she remembered the words her father had repeated so often: *God will give you back.* Never one to let a gift remain unacknowledged, she decided to give back to the uncle who had roused himself from heavenly peace to bring her a vision of the gift that was on its way into her arms. As she held little Wadi Edward she let out a tremulous sigh of relief. She and Issam had started their family with prayer and faith that she would be healed of her endometriosis. Their family was completed in the same way—with prayer and faith that they could trust whatever God had in store for them.

28

Don't Ever Doubt

It was late summer 2003. At this point in his career Dr. Nemeh had a well-established acupuncture practice and a public prayer ministry that was reaching about five hundred people each month. He had prayed over nearly twenty thousand people in the healing services that he had offered during the past two years. Yet between Issam and Kathy there was an unresolved issue that had only recently surfaced. Kathy was not yet participating in praying over people; she saw her roles in the healing services as being Issam's liaison as well as the visionary who made sure the healing services answered the needs of the people. Issam had a different view: he believed she was ready to join him in the prayer line. Kathy resisted. She was asking herself, *Who am I to pray over people?* rather than understanding, as Issam had been telling her since they first met, that the question she should be asking herself was *Who is God and what does He want from me?* It took a dramatic lesson for Kathy to understand what Issam was telling her.

Issam was in need of a vacation. Kathy asked his secretary, Carmie, to clear the schedule and planned a quick trip to Cancún for the whole family, departing from Cleveland in mid-August.

The water was beautiful and the hotel stay a wonderful respite. A few days after they arrived, however, the waves became so choppy that hotel management posted signs warning people not to swim in the ocean. Kathy and the kids settled in around the pool, but Issam continued walking toward the beach. "I'm going for a swim," he said, nonchalantly.

"Issam," Kathy objected. "Signs are posted everywhere! Just stay here with us."

"I can't swim in that used water," Issam said, gesturing dismissively toward the pool. He had grown up spending his summers in Latakia, swimming in the clear waters of the Mediterranean Sea.

Kathy and the kids watched him churn ever further from the shore. After he had been swimming for a time, he turned around and swam back to the shore. He trudged across the beach and over to the pool. He was aggravated.

"I lost my glasses," he said. Issam always kept his glasses on when he swam. "Does anyone have a pair of goggles I can borrow so I can look for them?"

His four children and his wife stared in dumbstruck silence.

Kathy found her voice. "You are kidding, aren't you?"

"No."

He looked at her as though she was the one asking the foolish question. "I've got to find my glasses."

"Issam, we'll go to an eyeglass store and get you a new pair. I'm sure there's a place right here that will make you a pair of glasses in a few hours."

Issam rolled his eyes, turned around without saying another word, and headed back out to the beach.

"Come on, kids," Kathy said, "let's go watch your father find his glasses."

"It's going to take more than St. Anthony to find them," Fadia observed drily. "It's going to take every available saint and angel."

The family followed Issam's footprints and stood in the wet sand at the edge of the sea, choppy waves slapping at their ankles. They watched him make his way out to the area in which he had been swimming when the Caribbean swallowed his glasses. They saw him dive down into the water once, stay below for an uncomfortably long amount of time, and bob back to the surface.

He made another dive. The waves frolicked above him.

Down, down, down he pushed, and as he dove he prayed, "Holy Spirit in the name of Jesus Christ . . ."

At that moment he saw a flash of light. He reached out toward the light and grabbed at it. His hand closed around the eyeglasses. He surged to the top and turned toward the shore. Triumphant, he waved his eyeglasses in an arc so that they could see he had found them.

The family stood transfixed as Issam swam back. Rising from the Caribbean like a sea creature and looking straight at Kathy with every step he took, his eyes burned a hole straight to her soul.

"*That* was for *you*."

She couldn't speak.

"That was for *you*, Kathy, so that you would *finally* see that God can do *anything*. Don't. Ever. Doubt."

At that moment Kathy realized the difference in their belief systems. For Issam, it was "believe it, and you will see it," rather than "see it, and you will believe it." After witnessing her husband's faith, she knew now she was being called upon to cast away her last vestige of doubt and view God's infinite abilities the way Issam saw them, with or without his eyeglasses.

Part Four

FAITH
AND
WORKS

29

The Emissary

Based on word-of-mouth referrals that kept the office phone ringing, the doctor was working six days a week at his acupuncture practice in 2007 and was helping thousands of patients in countless ways. Issam's faith and unflappable patience had inspired Kathy such that her faith had also become a powerful force for change, and the couple had achieved a complementary partnership in the public prayer ministry. In their work, Issam's forte was his one-on-one care of patients, while Kathy's extroverted personality equipped her to serve out in the community. If the doctor is like the axle of his practice and ministry, then Kathy is the wheel. Kathy's unique and spirited approach was demonstrated in the circumstances surrounding the birth of a friend's child in early 2007.

Shannon Cain, wife, mother, and president of Cain and Associates Investigative Accounts, turned to two physicians for her care throughout her pregnancy: Dr. David Eberlein, who would deliver her sixth child at Fairview General Hospital in Cleveland on March 1, 2007, and Dr. Nemeh, whose signature faith and reliance on prayers invoked in tandem with medical expertise helped Shannon all throughout her pregnancy. Kathy responded to Shannon's plaintive last-minute request for help and gave her support during the birth of Shannon's healthy baby boy.

Shannon's labor was artificially induced by means of intravenously administered Pitocin at 9:40 in the morning. Induced labor can go one of two ways. Some women respond well and deliver quickly, while others are more resistant to the drug and labor proceeds slowly. Shannon fell into the latter category. At seven that night Shannon's husband, Michael, who had been helpful and supportive all day long, found himself unable to quell the sense of panic building in his wife. So Shannon called Kathy, who happened to be driving across the Fairview Park bridge, a mere thirty seconds from the hospital. When Kathy said hello, the sound of her voice made Shannon lose her composure.

"Shanni—talk to me," Kathy said. "Is everything okay?"

"Can you start praying now?" Shannon said between sobs. "And can you come here to be with me?"

"I'm coming," Kathy assured her friend. She called Issam at the office as she drove to the hospital, and told him what was happening. He promised he would be praying for Shannon.

After practicing medicine for twenty-one years Dr. Eberlein still exulted upon delivering new life into the hands of parents. Even with his extensive experience, he was surprised when Shannon's friend joined them in the birthing room and, by virtue of her faith, sense of humor, and compassion, proved a first-rate birthing assistant.

Kathy was no doula; she certainly had never been trained in the birthing of a baby. On the other hand, she had become many things to Shannon: surrogate mother, sister, and confidante. They had become close ever since Shannon had suffered a miscarriage two years previously, and Dr. Nemeh had helped Shannon accept the loss as part of God's plan.

When in this, her seventh pregnancy, Shannon received an ominous report following her twenty-week ultrasound, warning that there was a high risk for chromosomal abnormality, she refused an amniocentesis on the basis that she would not consider ending the pregnancy no matter what happened. Instead she turned to Dr. Nemeh and was comforted. She also adopted as her mantra something Kathy had told her: *Surrender to the will of God.*

And now here she was, in the throes of the final stages of labor.

Dr. Eberlein performed an artificial rupture of the amniotic membranes, after which labor got very active very quickly. "For most women this is the worst part of labor," Dr. Eberlein later said. "It is especially so with a Pitocin-induced labor. The Pitocin often makes women feel a sense of captivity or of 'being done to,' but there was none of that for Shannon." Kathy's zany sense of humor distracted Shannon from the pain of transition. Dr. Eberlein had never seen anything quite like it. "I have attended births in Guatemala and Nigeria, where women endure labor in a personal sphere of quietude. Of course, labor in the United States is neither quiet nor celebratory no matter what anesthetic is utilized. But here was an incredible thing unfolding before me: a woman *laughing* through transition!"

Dr. Eberlein took a seat in a rocking chair and watched,

fascinated. "Kathy was larger than life and spiritually in-spired," he recalled some months after the birth. "She brought a different dimension into the room. Pain was treated with prayer. Prayer, when pain subsided, was replaced by laughter, which left a residue of joy."

The doctor fully endorses the Patch Adams philosophy of bringing humor and joy to medicine, most especially when people are in difficult situations. He said Kathy was living that philosophy to the fullest right there in front of his eyes in a way that he had never seen anyone do. "I was inspired to renew my commitment to bring lightheartedness—and prayerful-ness for those who wish—to each delivery," the doctor com-mented. "Being a participant in this memorable episode of love and spirituality in action gave me encouragement that this was surely the best way to practice medicine. I had been aware of these tools throughout my career, but never before had I seen them so beautifully enacted in the labor and delivery experi-ence."

Shannon felt the urge to push. Dr. Eberlein checked her and pronounced her almost ready to deliver but told her she could not push for another twenty minutes, after which he walked out of the room. Shannon looked to Kathy with terror, and her green eyes seemed to be asking: *How will I be able to do this? How can I resist the urge to push?*

An impish grin lit Kathy's face. She crouched like a catcher, rolled up her sleeves, and squared off. She laid out her plan. "Here's what we're going to do, Shanni. We're going to sur-prise the doctor. You're going to push, I'm going to deliver the baby—then *you and I* can split the fee!"

Kathy continued in her stand-up-comedienne act by point-ing to the nurse. "You have to cut the cord," she said with a wink. "I'll deliver the baby, but I'm *not* cutting any cord. I'm not even going to *look*." She rubbed her hands together and mischief danced in her eyes. "Okay, Shanni, let's *do it!*"

When Shannon burst into laughter, Kathy knew she had accomplished her goal of taking the edge off Shannon's panic. After Shannon's laughter subsided, Kathy pulled out her trump card: her rosary. "Okay, Shannon," Kathy said, "now we're going to pray." The two women stayed focused by calling on Blessed Mother for strength.

After Dr. Eberlein returned to the delivery room, he later recalled, "The birthing was blissfully uncomplicated and admirably well controlled. Shannon was able to push when she needed to push and refrain from pushing when necessary. She was fully alert, participatory, and able to share the quintessential moment of her baby's birth in a way that was unique among all her deliveries."

The nurse in attendance murmured, "What a beautiful birth," when little Stephen Michael slid out of the birth canal and into the hands of Dr. Eberlein. Kathy caught her breath; it all had happened so quickly. Feeling emotional, as he always did whenever he delivered life into this world, Dr. Eberlein placed the beautiful baby boy on Shannon's abdomen.

Thinking back on that day, Dr. Eberlein voiced one regret. He wished the labor and delivery had been videotaped. "The birth was filled with experiential wonderment. If you could design a whole birthing experience I don't think it could be done any better. I have seen people with equal joy—not many. A few very specially bonded mothers to daughters, an occasional father to daughter, an occasional husband to wife, able to share the experience, coach them through, and know exactly what they are going through. I haven't seen these people be able to sustain that joyous presence without becoming dismayed at some point or being drawn into their laboring loved one's pain. This was as loving an experience as I have ever seen, but it remained joyous. It was jubilant.

"It was absolutely about the baby. The baby was the focal point of the whole experience—that quintessential moment when this little life is delivered into the hands of his parents and greeted on earth.

"My wish for the world is that it could always be this way."

30.

Compassion

The lives and works of saints are typified by acts of compassion in which their extraordinary abilities are used to benefit others. Examples abound, but a few will illustrate the point.

Father Solanus Casey, a Capuchin priest who lived in friaries in Michigan and New York, was known the world over at the time of his death in 1957 as a wonder-worker whose prayers were associated with tens of thousands of miracles. At the monastery he was assigned the ignoble task of porter, the one who answered the door at the friary. While he was acting in that capacity, Father Solanus's attentive listening skills and compassion drew people to him, and many were blessed with healings and miracles after talking with this humble priest. More amazed than anyone at the manifestations of God's healing hand, Solanus would openly weep as heart disease, cancer, tuberculosis, blindness, polio, lameness, depression, alcoholism, insanity, and other conditions were cured right before his eyes.

In an attempt to disguise his gift of healing, St. Martin de

Porres of Peru pretended to utilize various props, such as fruit and herbs, when he prayed over the sick. For fifty years, during the late 1500s and early 1600s, Martin set a standard for service to the poor, homeless, orphaned, and sick. He turned his monastery into a food distribution center, clinic, and shelter. St. Martin ministered to the spiritual, physical, and educational needs of thousands even as he himself observed the strictest vows of poverty.

St. Francis of Assisi once was moved to place a kiss of compassion on the deformed face of a stranger, after which the man's face was restored to the way it had looked before it was ravaged by cancer.

St. Padre Pio, whose compassionate embrace of a lifeless six-month-old baby famously revived the child right before his mother's eyes, hid the joy he felt at the enactment of miracles behind a famously gruff exterior. Understanding that not everyone who sought his intervention would receive a miracle, Padre Pio raised funds and saw to fruition a vibrant world-class medical facility he named the "House for the Relief of Suffering," which opened in 1956. A phrase often repeated by Padre Pio summarizes what is at the core of all acts of compassion: "Love is the first ingredient in the relief of suffering."

Although saints strive to take away suffering from others, many welcome personal trials, discomfort, poverty, hunger, sickness, and pain for themselves. Why? They find a higher meaning in their pain. What they cannot abide in the lives of those they serve they accept for themselves. For example, many times Father Solanus was found asleep on the floor at the foot of the altar, having put a sick person in his own bed. St. Francis of Assisi eschewed a life of indulgence as the son of a wealthy merchant, turning instead to asceticism. St. Martin wore only the roughest of garments even as he gained widespread renown for clothing the poor. St. Padre Pio heard confessions and counseled penitents for fourteen hours a day and continued praying for these people—as many as thirty-four rosaries in one day, as well as lengthy prayers all throughout the night.

Dr. Nemeh would never consider himself a saint, and in recounting the stories of his life and career, he alludes to, but will not dwell on, the hard times he has endured. Certainly he has not turned his back on family and home to live a life of abject poverty, yet Dr. Nemeh's life journey has not been free of burdens.

History has shown, for example, that those belonging to religious minorities typically undergo some degree of persecution within their culture. One can imagine that growing up a Christian in a predominantly Muslim environment in Syria must have presented some challenges for young Issam.

Tradition also suggests that contemporaries can be quite critical of those dreamy individuals who, hearing a distant cadence, step outside the parade to pursue an altogether individual route. This might explain some of the ostracism within the medical field that can sometimes be experienced by a physician who insists on incorporating prayer, or, what he views as "the missing piece," in the holistic care of his patients.

Ministering to those who live in misery as part of one's calling typically causes a simpatico sharing of pain. Dr. Nemeh admits to this kind of suffering. Of the connection that is the healing path between God, the person over whom he is praying, and himself, he says, "I am oftentimes so connected with my patients via the Holy Spirit that I can feel the *physical changes* that are happening in their healings. The *emotional* part of my patients . . . yes, I feel their pain."

Indeed, many patients have validated his statement. Most striking are the testimonials given by victims of abuse. Some have confided that even though they did not reveal their past to Dr. Nemeh, he walked into the treatment room, tears immediately came to his eyes, and he wept silently. *How did he know?* they wonder. As the treatment session progressed, doctor and patient were often able to talk about the secret sorrows the abused patients had held inside.

Many patients perceive Dr. Nemeh's compassion as a dense, emotive, unconditional, and nonjudgmental act of love. The blessing they most appreciate is that some—and sometimes *all*—of their burdens are lifted when he prays for them.

Issam is "with the work," as he puts it, "from morning to morning." He reflects upon his place in the world: "I don't have a national identity. I cannot differentiate my family from anyone else anymore, because everybody is a family member. Anyone who belongs to the kingdom of God is my 'family.' The only difference, for me, is that God has entrusted this wife and these children to me, and it is my responsibility to help them survive in the world. My love for them is not bigger than my love for others. I belong to everybody when it comes to my service."

Nonetheless, Dr. Nemeh is a devoted husband and father, a man who leads with his heart and reaches out to protect his family at all times. For instance, in November 2007, nineteen-year-old Ashley was to sing a welcoming program at Mt. Zion Church of Oakwood Village. Although she was normally unflappable, for some reason she was overcome that day with a case of nerves. She sat quietly in a darkened corner.

Her hands, folded in her lap, were oddly still and her face was colorless. She stared into space, dark circles below her pretty brown eyes.

Her father was hurrying from the main presentation hall after having spoken with Charlene Kalo, who had catered the event and would also give the welcoming speech, and ushers Mary Dolan, Joanne Scudder, Maureen Leimkuehler, Diane Davie, Paula Kappos, and Vivian Costanzo, who would help more than a thousand people to their seats. He was needed over in a side room to answer questions the tech crew had about the PowerPoint presentation and videotaping of the event. As he passed the musicians, keyboard accompanist Patty Zinn reached out and touched Issam on the arm. "I think your daughter could use a prayer," she said in a low voice and pointed to Ashley in the shadows. Issam's head turned sharply in the direction the musician was pointing and in an instant his expression melted from all business to all compassion. "Oh," he breathed, and then called her by name.

She looked up. A light flickered in her eyes, animating a face that just a moment ago had appeared expressionless. She stood and faced him. Issam extended his hands over his sweet girl, closed his eyes, and prayed. Ashley bowed her head beneath the protective umbrella of her father's prayer. The two were motionless for several minutes.

Their eyes opened simultaneously. Ashley smiled at her father. She looked like a different person. The dark circles were gone. Color flooded her cheeks.

She took the stage, sang a set list of inspirational songs accompanied by the Mount Zion musicians with backing vocals sung by the Mount Zion gospel choir, and inspired a crowd of twelve hundred.

————

The Nemehs are a close family, one that has fun together and laughs a lot. Although Issam is by nature a serious man, when one of the children can make their father laugh—his laughter is characteristically subdued, coming alive more in his eyes than in his voice—it's as though she or he has won a prize. Maybe it's because so often they can see sorrow pressing down on his spirit.

The specific challenges Dr. Nemeh has faced matter less than his life philosophy for dealing with adversity. In this, he has adopted an approach similar to that of the saints and the prayerful: he seizes upon bad times as golden opportunities. Dr. Nemeh says, "Suffering is *joy*. I become a *better* spiritual being when I suffer. It becomes a beautiful opportunity, and I become a different spiritual being. I thank God for the opportunity He is giving me to shine more and more for Him." When a physical healing eludes a patient, Dr. Nemeh is able to offer an authentic perspective that this suffering is part of God's plan. As such, it should be embraced as an opportunity to shine for God.

31

As Above, So Below

Spending so many hours at his practice and healing services, Dr. Nemeh has very little free time. Once in a while he will meander around a grocery store or shopping mall with Kathy and the kids, and occasionally the family will go out for dinner together. Going to a sports event never crosses his mind. In 2005 WEWS News Channel 5 conducted a survey of the fifty most interesting people in Cleveland. Ted Henry called Kathy Nemeh with the results of the poll, saying, "Dr. Nemeh was voted the third most interesting person to Clevelanders." When Kathy told her husband of this honor, Issam responded with a shrug of his shoulders, muttering something about not understanding what the big deal was all about.

Then Kathy asked, "Guess who's the first most interesting person to Clevelanders?"

Playing along, Issam replied, "Who?"

"LeBron James." At the age of eighteen LeBron James was already considered a basketball superstar and had been selected by the Cleveland Cavaliers as the first pick in the 2003 National Basketball Association draft. Cavaliers fans rejoiced, believing that James's talent would prove to be the salvation of the struggling franchise. All throughout northeast Ohio, hero worship of LeBron James was in evidence.

Although Kathy realizes her husband is immured in a world of work and prayer, even she was surprised when Issam tilted his head and wondered aloud, "Who is LeBron James?"

What Dr. Nemeh has gained from years of living in faith is the secret to getting into heaven. His life's work, in one sense, is about sharing this insight with as many people as he can. He believes, as did Jesus, Buddha, the saints and mystics, that the gates to heaven are unlocked with love—love for God and love of others. All of us can incorporate love into our lives so that we, too, will someday turn the key that admits us into heaven. How do we do this?

Because perfection exists only in God, Dr. Nemeh says, we can begin our journey of faith with confidence that God is not looking for perfect love from us. What He seeks is our free will decision *to love.*

"When you say 'love' a barrage of other things apply," says Dr. Nemeh. "Patience. Endurance. Persistence. The ability to withstand attack. A willingness to change. An eagerness to love God. Love entails everything good.

"We are living in the New Testament era where the perfection of our works is not what will restore us to heaven, but rather the perfect grace of God. St. James wrote that just as a body without spirit is dead, faith without works is lifeless. So first faith, then works."

Dr. Nemeh believes that "God models everything for us so that we can understand His design." Thus, in his view, God has faith first: He has faith in *us.* He has faith that we *want* Him. He sustains the turning of the world based on His faith that we desire and struggle toward fulfillment, which we intuit will be achieved at our reunification with Him.

It follows, then, that His works come after His faith, too.

The works God displays to sustain our imperfect faith are the manifestations of the action-oriented Holy Spirit.

What exactly is the Holy Spirit?

Issam describes the essence of the Spirit in one word: "verb." "The Holy Spirit is the active part of the Trinity. In fact, the Holy Spirit is the activator and the perfecting of the relationship between the Father and the Son, as well as the way by which we complete *our* relationship with the Father." The reason that people over whom Dr. Nemeh prays experience unusual physiological changes, such as a rush of intense heat or falling backward into the outstretched arms of a catcher, is that the Spirit is actively intervening. So, too, the Spirit is the way by which healings from God are accomplished. It is the Spirit who is responsible for all the "manifesting" people see and feel at healing services. These interventions, Dr. Nemeh says, are the reenactment between humans and God of the same perfecting activity that connects the Father and Son. As above, so below.

For Dr. Nemeh, God created us so that our humanity might be a reflection of the Trinity. "God made it easy for us," says Issam. "We know He created man according to His own image and likeness. Well, who are we? We have a mind, a body, and a spirit. There it is: the Trinity.

"The Hebrew word for 'spirit' is *ruach*—a feminine image," Issam explains. "The only translation that was possible in ancient times was the male gender. But 'spirit' in Hebrew is feminine in the same way that 'sky' is feminine. It makes sense that the Spirit has a female quality because the woman is the conduit by which every son is born.

"This is the beacon for me: the perfection and the love between Father and Son via the Spirit. It guided me toward my own connection with the Father. For me, it's a total surrender to the will of God. This is an age-old concept. It is the Judeo concept. Everything is there in the Jewish religion. It is complete . . . except for the one thing everyone was waiting for: the manifestation, the sign, the anointed one, the Messiah. Jesus.

"Love is the main attribute of God, and love is what holds together the Trinity. The Spirit is the passion—the firestorm of love that *binds* Father to Son, and Trinity to *us*. The Spirit connected the Son and the Father. Again, as above, so below: the Trinity models how it should be for God's children. It shows that the way for us to reconnect with the Father is through the Holy Spirit. All we have to do is imitate the lovingness modeled by the Spirit."

That model is the basis for the healing services, which he says provide a public display of God's grace and love. As such, they are proof of God's very real involvement in our lives. Dr. Nemeh says the public manifestations are happening more frequently and dramatically now than ever before because the urgency of the times has created a great yearning for meaning, a desire for connectedness to something greater than ourselves.

When people come to a service, Issam recognizes that one of three types of healings might happen. First, people might receive a healing. Second, people might receive a partial healing—which may or may not prove to be the jumping-off point for a spiritual journey. Third, people might witness someone else's healing. The point of all three possibilities, says Dr. Nemeh, is that these are signs that make people stop, ponder God, and consider the role they allow God to play in their lives.

At the heart of Dr. Nemeh's career are "manifestations." Put simply, manifestations are physical, emotional, and spiritual changes that occur with faith, prayer, and connection. When Dr. Nemeh prayed over a three-year-old boy and a tumor disappeared from his face, the disappearance of the tumor was a manifestation. When a paraplegic regained her ability to walk while Dr. Nemeh was praying, this was another manifestation. When cancerous kidney tumors vanish after prayers with Dr. Nemeh, this, too, is a manifestation.

A manifestation. Otherwise known as a miracle.

≺ᴪ

The "M" Word

In July 2009 Joe Kuty drove coworker Sharon Deitrick to Dr. Nemeh's office. Although Sharon knew the doctor had recently implemented a trial program of remote prayer sessions via telephone and the Internet, she scheduled an in-office acupuncture treatment four days before the surgical removal of a mass on her left kidney. Her relative Scott met them there.

Sharon found out about the kidney quite by accident when her doctor ordered a CAT scan to rule out colon cancer as the cause of internal bleeding. The test film was sent to both of her internists as well as to the oncologist who had treated her for endometrial cancer years earlier. The diagnosis for the internal bleeding was stress-induced colitis, but the scan also revealed a sizeable mass on a very enlarged left kidney.

Sharon came to Dr. Nemeh on the strength of three recommendations. First, there were the things her friend Chris had said about her experience with the doctor four years previously. Chris had come to the doctor for treatment of a brain tumor. Sharon was eager to know how the appointment had gone. Chris told her, "Sharon, he was *wonderful*." Yet as Chris recounted what had happened it was clear this was not the kind of wonderful outcome for which Sharon was hoping. Chris continued, "He wept when he saw me, so I knew right away that it was not for me to be here much longer. Still, he gave me the peace of mind to be able to prepare for heaven. I told him how concerned I was about my children and my husband, and he made me feel so much better. He told me not to be afraid." In 2005 Chris died in a state of easy, peaceful grace.

In January 2009 Sharon's relative Scott experienced an amazing healing with one visit to Dr. Nemeh. Scott had sustained a perforated disc during a spinal tap to rule out bacterial meningitis. This injury set off a chain of events: brain fluid compensated by dripping into the spine. The brain structure dropped within the cranium, where it was caught by the optic nerves. There it rested, putting pressure on nerves not designed to support the weight of a brain. He lay in bed in agony, unable to lift his head from the pillow. On Super Bowl Sunday he returned to the hospital, where doctors attempted to patch the hole; brain surgery was discussed as a possible course of action. With one treatment from Dr. Nemeh, Scott was restored to health; brain surgery was no longer necessary.

In mid-July 2009 Sharon attended a Dr. Nemeh healing service at St. Michael the Archangel Catholic Church in Canton, Ohio. Her intention was to collect a prayer in absentia on behalf of her sister, Cookie, who lived in Washington, D.C. Colorectal cancer, hemorrhaging, lymphoma, and new masses on her breast had left Cookie so weakened that her other sisters, who were by her side, called Sharon and whispered, "We're afraid we're really going to lose her." Sharon learned later that Cookie improved almost precisely at the minute when Dr. Nemeh stood before Sharon and prayed for Cookie.

Sharon, thinking that the doctor's prayer for Cookie was the end of her moment with Dr. Nemeh, was flabbergasted when he reached around to her back, put his hand over her left kidney, and began a new prayer. She wondered, *How in the world could he have discerned this diseased organ?*

The prayer for her sister in absentia along with the unsolicited prayer over her kidney were the final two prompts that compelled Sharon to make an appointment with the doctor after the CAT scan revealed the presence of a large mass on her left kidney. Sharon came to Dr. Nemeh's Rocky River office hoping that God wished to grant a miracle for her.

She felt shy about having Scott and Joe in the room during her treatment, so they settled into chairs in the waiting room. As soon as she entered the treatment room Sharon changed her mind. "It was immediately obvious to me there was grace in that room. I thought, *It is not for me to be selfish. I should not prevent the others from sharing this grace.*" She asked if they might come in, and Dr. Nemeh indicated it would be fine. Scott and Joe joined them.

Within five minutes of beginning his acupuncture treatment, Dr. Nemeh reassured her, "Do not be afraid of your kidney surgery. They will not find anything there."

Dr. Nemeh then directed his attention to her legs. He grasped her "bad leg" and began to move it into a proper position. Sharon said, "Oh, no, Dr. Nemeh—that leg cannot move that way." She had contracted a form of polio in childhood and her bone structure had been abnormal ever since.

Dr. Nemeh just smiled and continued his manipulation of the leg. As he did so, Sharon heard a sound that was rather like the coarse grinding of ice cubes being dispensed from a refrigerator. Joe, who wears a hearing aid, exclaimed, "Oh my *God!* Do you *hear* that?" Although Sharon could hear the sound of her bones being moved, she felt no pain.

Dr. Nemeh stood and moved behind Sharon's chair. He put two fingers on her shoulder. Instantly Sharon, Joe, and Scott heard a rapid-fire clackety-clacking, like a train running over tracks, starting at her neckline and descending all the way down her back—the biological equivalent of a brilliant glissando tumbling down a piano keyboard.

"That was fast," commented Dr. Nemeh more to himself than anyone. "Your vertebrae just realigned," he explained. Then he asked, "Your abdomen is numb, isn't it?"

"Yes," she answered, startled. "How do you know that?" Hardly anyone knew about the numbness that remained after two endometrial cancer surgeries, one performed sixteen years and the other ten years earlier. When he probed that area, she could feel the doctor's fingers on skin that had been completely numb for more than a decade.

During the treatment Joe and Scott noticed an otherworldly expression of bliss on Sharon's face. Twice the doctor spoke to her but she didn't answer. The men later told her she looked as if she was in a trance. For Sharon, that time felt euphoric. It felt almost as if she were floating in a sea of ecstasy.

Dr. Nemeh looked out the small window as he worked. His gaze skipped past the ugly flat rooftop of the next-door office building and lighted instead on some rays of sunshine. He smiled. "The light from heaven defies all laws of disease."

Then he shared a little of his unique perspective with the trio.

"I see you the way God sees you. I see the beauty of the

person the way you are *meant* to be—the way you are *going* to be—after God transforms you."

He started to tell them how he was able to discern so many medical conditions with what seemed to be X-ray vision. He said, "If you become one in the Spirit with Christ, then you move with the Spirit. I go where the Holy Spirit tells me to go."

When Sharon expressed gratitude, he smiled and replied, "Don't thank me. Thank Jesus. I have no skill. I am merely God's donkey."

On July 28, Sharon entered the operating room feeling strangely happy. She told the surgical team, "All of you are being prayed for today, so do not worry." Then she asked, "Have any of you heard of Dr. Nemeh?" She paused but her question was met with silence. She continued. "Well, I went to him, and he told me not to be afraid. He said you would not find anything on my kidney." As she spoke these words she could see the CAT scan image of her kidney projected on a monitor positioned up high, so that the medical team could refer to it during surgery. She also could see their faces as they rolled their eyes. Nevertheless, Sharon felt at peace. "I felt confident," she recalled a couple of weeks after the surgery. "Confident that God had touched me through the hands of Dr. Nemeh, and confident from the power of prayers prayed by so many on my behalf." She requested a mild form of anesthesia, knowing recovery would be much easier that way than if a general anesthetic were administered.

Sharon was still in the operating room when she awakened.

There in the glare of the bright lights, the surgeon told her something she already knew. "The mass is gone," he said.

"You got it all?" Sharon asked.

"No. It was gone. There was nothing there. I even flushed your kidney and it is working beautifully. We did not even have to place a stent in your kidney."

Pushing for the point, Sharon dared to use "the 'm' word" in that revered medical science setting. "So. It was a miracle."

"It must have been because I have no explanation," the surgeon said.

As one of the attendant nurses wheeled Sharon to recovery, he was forthcoming in sharing what had happened that day. He used a word that struck a nerve, and she knew she would always remember what he said. He said, "We were *stupefied*."

He went on. "At one point we were looking at the screen at a kidney that was all swollen and had a large mass on it. Then during the procedure, we saw no swelling . . . no blockage . . . no mass." He fell silent for a moment as he thought back on his experience.

"We even used the forbidden word in the operating room."

"So—do you believe?" she asked.

"I do believe," he replied. "I witnessed it today."

For Dr. Nemeh, the manifestations—the miracles—are like sign language. To those blessed with an unexplainable cure, they are the means by which God communicates. They are proof of the presence of One who walks beside us and hears our prayers.

"We can believe," says Dr. Nemeh, "because we have seen. God's intention with the manifestations is to fortify the faith of His children. To work miracles in our own lives, we must follow this plan: have only love in our hearts, and proceed with first faith, then works. In order for the door to heaven to open to us, we must trust that God is love, that love is what He intends for us, and love is what He wants from us. Then, through loving-kindness, we will make our way toward Him."

33

The Journeyman

At five in the morning on Christmas Day 2003, Kathy was awakened by the sound of Issam talking in his sleep. He was speaking in Aramaic. Heart pounding, she listened and soon realized she was hearing one side of a conversation. When the dialogue was finished Issam moaned and said, in English, "I was not allowed to go."

At precisely the same time, someone's loud exhale awakened Philip Keller from his sleep. A vision appeared in his mind that showed him what he was hearing: it was the sound of Issam's last earthly breath. As the vision unfolded Philip heard the name of Jesus being spoken in Issam's voice and then a choir singing.

Shaken, Philip got out of bed. He descended the stairs, feeling like he was in a dream. It was so real, so vivid, Philip was convinced the vision was a premonition, and that it was true. He sat in the quiet of the living room in the barely visible glow from hundreds of tiny white lights on the fireplace mantel and Christmas tree. His hands were ice cold and he was suffused with sadness so thick it seemed to suffocate his heart and soul. In the room that awaited Christmas joy he cried and began talking to himself, reasoning out what he had seen. He knew that he was battling his own belief system. *This vision was too real to be nothing. But——I would have heard something by now. Kathy would have called.* He forced himself to wait until a seemly hour before telephoning the Nemehs, wishing everyone a Merry Christmas, and asking if everything was okay. He was relieved to hear everything was fine.

Philip arrived at the office for his regular appointment with Dr. Nemeh the following Tuesday, nervously anticipating how he would bring up his Christmas vision. Kathy greeted him in the waiting room with a smile. "How are you, Philip? How was your Christmas?"

Agitated, he blurted out, "Did anything happen at around five o'clock on Christmas morning?"

"Oh my God..." said Kathy softly. "Philip, I was awakened, too, at the same time." They traded stories.

At that point in their conversation Issam came out of the treatment room and his patient departed. Philip told Issam about his Christmas morning premonition. Kathy watched Issam carefully. Issam seemed surprised and a little bemused that God had given Philip a glimpse of Issam's Christmas morning experience.

Issam answered, "You were experiencing some of what I was going through, my friend."

Then, with an expression of ineffable sadness in his eyes, he said, "I wanted to go; I wanted to follow Jesus. But I was not allowed. He told me I had to stay."

Some weeks later, Issam felt as though his health was deteriorating; he had been working very hard for so long. The thought occurred to him: *I'm going to go today.* When he fell into his bed that Saturday night he sank into a deep sleep. Again he dreamed of being with Jesus.

He dreamed that after his final patient of the day departed, he cleaned the treatment room, sank heavily into the reclining chair, and closed his eyes in prayer. Hovering between prayer and sleep, he felt the Holy Spirit descend. The elongated chair changed into a canoe, and the Dove's wings became paddles propelling them through calm waters.

The boat settled into an easy pace. Issam enjoyed the beautiful rocks and silver fish he saw below the surface. He looked to the riverbank because his attention had been caught by a graceful tree with overarching branches skimming the water. He noticed that along the riverbank were multitudes of people. It was the same on the other side of the river. He realized with a start that the people were looking at *him.*

Overcome with shyness, he averted his eyes. *This is strange,* he thought. When he raised his eyes again the people were still staring at him. He tried to understand what this was all about. It began to sink in that he knew these folks. He looked at one face, then the next and the next and discovered that each was familiar. They were either hospital patients or people he had treated in his office, or people he had prayed over. Some were smiling; some were not. He recalled their names and their healing journeys. He recognized tens of thousands of faces.

The canoe began to pick up speed.

The water splashed in his face.

He closed his eyes, tilted his head up toward heaven, and laughed.

The Dove's wings whistled as they pumped. The riverbanks swelled, and it was as if the earth, grass, and foliage were on wheels and a stage crew of giants was rolling them forward, transforming the river into a new road. The faces of his patients fell away until each became just a grain of sand. Within a matter of moments, then, the canoe was racing at breakneck speed, like a bobsled on an icy run. The canoe was now taking treacherous, flying turns over sand.

As the Dove and Issam hurtled along, Issam glimpsed moments in history, as though he was passing by dozens of gigantic outdoor theaters, with a minute or two to view the scenes playing across the screens. In one scene he watched as St. Paul was lowered over Bab Kisan, one of the seven ancient city gates of Damascus, in a basket, escaping certain death. In another he saw into Padre Pio's darkened confessional at the moment of transverberation, when a seraph threw a mystical dart of love and the future saint's soul was set on fire with love for God. He also watched as Pope Pius IX muscled the concept of papal infallibility into the First Vatican Ecumenical Council in 1870, and Issam's heart sank. Then he witnessed as, one century later, Pope John XXIII removed from the Church attic the cobweb-crusted concept of pope, bishops, and priests as servants and returned the Church to the people. Issam saw men and women of peace marching in a long parade of sorrows. He watched men and women of letters bent over parchment, typewriters, and computer keyboards spilling out words they hoped would turn the key of insight once and for all on poverty, suffering, and man's inhumanity to man. He glimpsed the knowledge of evil nearing completion and humanity inching precipitously closer to the belief that they, like God, could create. The boat continued flying past this survey of the world until Issam could not process any more, so full to breaking was his heart.

Just then the Holy Dove rearranged her wings and pointed her brilliant gaze toward the heavens. Up, up went the canoe, faster and faster until the sand fell away beneath them. Now they were gliding on polished clouds. The beauty of the celestial world eased Issam's heartache a little and he was able to relax his death grip on the sides of the boat.

After a time he felt the canoe slowing. Issam was surprised to see a mountain far off in the distance. The canoe coasted to a stop and rocked gently on a billowy cloud the color of moonlit snow. Before him were thousands of white-robed people. He immediately felt conspicuous because he knew he was dressed in his all-black office garb. He said a prayer: *Holy Spirit, let me know what you want of me.* The Spirit answered by clothing Issam in a white robe, and Issam understood he was to disembark from the canoe. He turned to express his gratitude but the Spirit had already flown away.

Issam studied the scene before him.

People walked in a single-file line that meandered up a mountainside. At the midpoint stood a figure. The white-robed pilgrims funneled around him like water around a great rock in the middle of a river, forming into a single line again when they had passed by.

Insight exploded into Issam's brain. *That's Jesus!*

His gaze darted to the pinnacle, where he saw Saints Peter and Paul.

This is heaven! All these people are going to heaven!

Issam was dizzy with ecstasy. *I've got to get into heaven.*

Heart pounding, he corrected himself: *I know Jesus will not let me. I just know He won't.*

An idea occurred to him. Feeling sneaky, like a truant,

he tried to hide himself within the crowd. He fell into line, shrunk down into the white robe, and began a stealthy, furtive hike up the mountain. When he reached the point where the line broke into two he marched to the left. He held his breath as he came abreast of Jesus. He was one step past Him; now two steps. The suspense was excruciating. His heart was thrumming. Now three steps . . .

He felt a mighty hand grab his collar and yank him backward. Suddenly he was no longer in the single-file line.

"No, son," Jesus told him. "You stand right here."

Issam stood beside his Lord. Sadness crashed down upon him. He did not know such an enormous grief was possible. He did not complain nor did he argue; he just felt sad.

After a few moments of watching the souls in their journey to Heaven, Jesus said, "You have a lot more work to do. You must go back."

Jesus turned from watching the heavenly procession. Issam saw reflected in His eyes the many souls that were waiting for the prayerful touch of Issam's hands.

"Here," said Jesus, and he extended His hands toward Issam.

Issam cupped upturned palms together. Jesus placed within them a gift. Still looking into Jesus' eyes, Issam closed his hands over the gift. He felt a small heart beating wildly, a heart that mirrored his own. Curious, Issam wrested his gaze from Jesus' eyes, parted his thumbs, and peeked inside. Therein sat a beautiful brown sparrow whose round black eyes seemed to be holding Issam's own past within their depths.

Issam once again raised his gaze to Jesus. He understood. This was not really a sparrow. It was *sadness*. It was his yearning to be with Jesus.

He knew what he had to do.

Issam stroked the little bird's soft head. He cradled this sorrow for a few moments. He raised the bird to his lips and gave it a kiss.

Then he looked into those Infinite Eyes and, opening his hands, let the sparrow go.

Acknowledgments

Like animals that are both nocturnal and diurnal, writers live in two different worlds. There is the introverted isolation of the writing process. There is also the extroverted world of camaraderie—the behind-the-scenes sustenance of family and friends that feeds the soul. Throughout the journey of writing this book, I have been sustained by the love of many, and gratitude is the feeling that best defines me these days.

A generous portion of my thankfulness belongs to Dr. Issam and Kathy Nemeh and their children, Fadia, Ashley, Debbie, and Wadi, who welcomed me into their home and lives and entrusted me with their stories. The one-on-one hours spent with Issam were exceptional; it was my privilege to sit beside this man and have him share with me some of the treasures of his profundity. Kathy was terrific about introducing me to contacts and tireless about answering my many questions. She opened up her world to me and ensured I was able to move with complete freedom within the ministry.

Without Charlene Kalo's matchmaking this book might

genius of a visionary, he helped me chisel and sculpt until the true shape of the narrative was freed from a dense and cumbersome block.

Without Gary Jansen, this book would have been merely a dream. Because of Gary, it's a dream come true.

never have been written. After having read an unpublished work of mine, Charlene was convinced I would be able to convey the essence of Dr. Nemeh's work; I am grateful to Charlene for the role she played in connecting me and the Nemehs.

I feel tremendous gratitude toward the volunteers and patients who offered their perspectives on Dr. Nemeh and his work and who shared their deeply personal stories in the hopes that others might benefit from their experiences. Special thanks must go to Shannon Cain and Sharon DeSanto, who were incredibly selfless in sharing their stories. I am appreciative of Philip Keller's tireless reminiscing, which helped me to understand the history of the ministry. Regretfully, not every personal journey was able to be recounted in these pages; I like to think they are present in spirit, between the lines. I am especially thankful to have met the late Jim Lyle, an amazingly courageous man, and his family, whose friendship I will always treasure.

I am very grateful to Bishop Roger Gries and the priests and clergy who took time from their busy schedules to share with me their informed point of view about Dr. Nemeh's public prayer ministry. I owe special thanks to Father Joseph Fata for his extraordinary hospitality in allowing me to shadow him, and to Father Dan Schlegel for arranging an interview session that was unforgettable.

To John Randall, my Bible coach, I owe undying gratitude for his courage in guiding a novice on her exploratory climb up the mountain of scriptural insight. To his wife, my fellow writer Dawn Neely-Randall, I give loving thanks for having been my first reader and constant cheerleader. As I wrote this book, these newlyweds were counting every minute together under the special circumstances of John living with a diagnosis of terminal lung cancer. The unmeasured sharing of their time is humbling.

Kathy Wainwright, my staunch friend for more than twenty years, celebrated each happy accomplishment with me all along my writing journey. She also intervened with uncannily prescient timing at moments of great stress. Her friendship, wisdom, and steadfastness throughout were blessings.

The contagious excitement and unwavering support shown me by Tim Moore, Ronald Lane, Mary Ellen Brock, and Kim Miraldi is heartwarming, and I thank them for having delighted in my amazing journey from writer to author.

I am deeply grateful to Patrick Coleman for his full-bodied storytelling, rescuing compassion during times of frustration, and loyalty that is the defining quality of an enduring Irish friendship.

Randy Zinn supported this project by performing computer triage and with his prayers and poems. (Even so, I like Randy for who he is, rather than for what he can do.) Randy also led me to my incredible Web design team and I cannot thank Kevin Marquart, Michelle Walsh, Brent Plesmid, and Ryan Garfield enough for believing in me and for turning my visions of a logo and a Web site into realities.

I promised Chuck Smolko when I began writing the book that I would not give up on my guitar lessons if he would not give up on me, and he didn't. More important, Chuck never added to my stress by making me feel guilty about unpracticed lessons.

I would have been a physical wreck without the personal training and Muscle Activation Technique therapy given me by

Ted Nicola and Kim Dakin Brody. I am grateful to them for strength & stamina, biceps & triceps, and 'bows & toes story time.

I am indebted to Mary and Mark Gigliotti and their daughters for friendship and prayers and for sharing their backyard retreat; I'll never forget my many hours writing outside, on the patio, under the spell of the ethereal beauty of their waterfall.

It meant a great deal to me that my brother, Gavin Poston, suspended his skepticism out of respect for my intellect and judgment and submitted to a personal spiritual passage through Dr. Nemeh's ministry. His candid and astute reflections were the source of many helpful conversations about my work.

Even though we were separated by nearly two thousand miles, Suzy Poston Navarro did her best to walk beside me every step of the way. Her belief in and encouragement of me is second only to the unconditional love and support I received all my life from my parents.

My family, quite simply, amazes me. The devotion shown by my daughter, Jackie, takes my breath away, for whether she was completing graduate studies, immersed in her fledgling career, or raising Keiran Siobhan, whose loveliness lights our lives, Jackie answered my every request for research assistance and critical reading. All my children supported me, each in his or her way, and I am deeply touched by their pride in my endeavor. I turned to Brittany for advice more times than I can count, and when my confidence flagged, hers was the voice I heard whispering in my ear, saying, *You can do it, Mom!* Rob was my cheerful technical assistant, new music advisor, and surrogate Donovan-walker. Juli was a tireless listener whenever I needed to ramble about my work, vent about my challenges, or flesh out new ideas. Connor and Dillon were forgiving of the thousands of hours when my work took precedence over our usual family routine. The love of sons-in-law Dave Merriman and Justin Stark for my daughters was liberating, because knowing that Jackie and Brittany are happy and safe is a precious gift of peace of mind.

To my husband, Eric, whose encouragement is unfailing and belief in my abilities abiding, I say thank you for everything—most especially for inviting me to the Elyria High School Talent Show. Who would have guessed on our first date that we would someday be enthralled by the real-life talent show of our own six children?

From the first, my beacon was the nonfiction narrative writing of Alex Kotlowitz, and I thank him for seminal works that are lighthouses guiding us toward greater empathy and compassion.

Copy editor Maggie Carr carried out her assignment as carefully as if it were her own book. I am indebted to her for the meticulous perfectionism she lavished on my work.

For the miracle of this book having been published by Doubleday Religion, Mary Ann Winkowski has my perpetual gratitude; she provided the fateful connection between a mother of six and the brilliant religion editor who would champion my project. And here is where I break down, for mere words cannot convey the profound gratitude I feel toward Gary Jansen, my editor.

It is my great blessing that Gary glimpsed the vein of something beautiful running through my massive original manuscript. Then, with ineffable patience, selfless generosity, and the